Perspectives on
BLUE ECONOMY

Perspectives on
BLUE ECONOMY

Vijay Sakhuja

Kapil Narula

National
Maritime
Foundation

Vij Books India
Pvt Ltd

New Delhi

Published by

Vij Books India Pvt Ltd
(Publishers, Distributors & Importers)
2/19, Ansari Road
Delhi – 110 002
Phones: 91-11-43596460, 91-11-47340674
Fax: 91-11-47340674
e-mail: vijbooks@rediffmail.com
we b: www.vijbooks.com

Copyright © 2017, *National Maritime Foundation*

First Published : 2017

ISBN: 978-93-85563-98-0 (Hardback)

ISBN: 978-93-85563- 99-7 (ebook)

Foreword

Oceans cover more than 70 per cent of the surface of the earth and provide valuable biological and mineral resources. Nearly 90 per cent of the worlds trade transits over the seas and this activity provides livelihood to a large number of people. Over time it has also been realised that healthy oceans are essential for a healthy planet and oceans need to be utilized sustainably.

The concept of 'Blue Economy' is therefore gaining momentum and is being actively discussed at various forums. The Blue Economy can also be interpreted as 'ocean economy' with its constituent sectors such as fishing, oil and gas, shipping and its associated activities including ship building, repair and port infrastructure, marine tourism and recreation. The concept has now become a driver for economic growth leading to sustainable development. India is essentially a maritime nation with a natural outflow towards the sea. With its Exclusive Economic Zone (EEZ) of more than 2.0 million square kilometers and a coastline of over 7500 kilometers, India has immense maritime interests and is aptly suited to harness the potential of the Blue Economy.

The National Maritime Foundation as India's leading maritime think tank, has been in the forefront of developing a policy prescriptive discourse on the Blue Economy. To arrive at a common understanding of the concept, the National Maritime Foundation is hosting its flagship event, the Annual Maritime Power Conference – 2017 on the theme: "The Blue Economy: Concept, Constituents and Development".

This volume is a compilation of a number of essays penned by the faculty of the Foundation and presents the authors perspectives on various aspects of the Blue Economy. The primary purpose is to provide a broad view on the Blue Economy among the academic community and the public at large with an aim to simulate further discussions. I am sure that this book will add to the existing literature and would go a long way in focusing attention on the oceans which have a vast potential to harness the 'Blue Economy'.

Admiral RK Dhowan, PVSM, AVSM, YSM (Retd.)
Chairman, National Maritime Foundation

Contents

Introduction

Oceans are an important source of a variety of living and non-living resources such as fish, off-shore oil, natural gas and minerals. They also contribute significantly to a country's GDP by facilitating trade and associated activities such as shipping, shipbuilding, ship repair and port operations along with generating employment opportunities throughout the maritime supply chain.

At another level, oceans are a major contributor of non-economic goods and ecosystem services and are central to life on earth. They provide oxygen, act as a heat sink and absorber of carbon dioxide and are an integral part of the weather system. Although oceans have been treated as an inexhaustible source of resources and an infinite sink, there is a growing realisation of the importance of healthy oceans for life on earth.

The rising importance of ocean based resources has resulted in the emergence of the term 'Blue Economy'. There is no universally accepted definition of the term, but it can be understood as the "integration of ocean economy development with the principles of social inclusion, environmental sustainability and innovative dynamic business models". Interestingly, the Blue Economy addresses both, resource scarcity and waste disposal systemically enhance human development in a holistic manner. The ecosystem approach helps to ensure that the physical environment, resources, and biodiversity are treated as intrinsically interconnected, underpin the concept and practice of Blue Economy.

The Blue Economy also presents several opportunities for growth in sectors such as biotechnology, desalination, port led development, sustainable fishing, mariculture and aquaculture, harnessing oceanic biodiversity and genetic resources, coastal and island tourism, ocean based renewable energy and seabed mining.

Given the manifold strength of the Blue Economy, its development is finding resonance amongst international and regional organisations such as the United Nations, African Union (AU), European Union (EU), Indian Ocean Rim Association (IORA), Asia Pacific Economic Cooperation (APEC), South Asian Association for Regional Cooperation (SAARC), which have adopted ocean based growth as an important agenda for cooperation, growth and prosperity. The Blue Economy is equally relevant to both, coastal and island states as also for land locked states. Small Island Developing States (SIDS) such as Mauritius, Seychelles, Maldives and bigger countries such as Bangladesh and India have supported the Blue Economy in different forums and are proactively engaged in promoting its development.

This volume is a collection of articles which presents the multidimensional aspects of the Blue Economy. The first section, deals with definitions and the interpretation of the Blue Economy and highlight the key principles. The relevance of Sustainable Development Goal (SDG) 2030 and SDG 14 which is related to the oceans is also discussed. Marine spatial planning which encourages multiple uses of the ocean is a key aspect for the implementation of the Blue Economy.

Sustainable use of marine resources and development of marine infrastructure for implementing the Blue Economy is discussed in the next two sections. Major issues of debate in this section are sustainable exploitation of fisheries, and combatting Illegal, Unreported and Unregulated (IUU) fishing. Further, renewable energy from oceans forms an important component of clean energy and India's endeavours to harness this potential is presented. Marine infrastructure and transport form an important component of blue growth and green ports, port infrastructure development and marine tourism industry offers many opportunities to harness the Blue Economy.

The next section focuses on environmental protection at sea and highlights the threats to the marine environment from shipping and plastics. It also analyses the implications of the forthcoming implementation of the ballast water management convention and the recent decisions of the International Maritime Organisation (IMO) towards strengthening environmental compliance at sea.

The role of international cooperative approaches for harnessing the Blue Economy is discussed in the penultimate section. International developments for adopting the concept of Blue Economy, establishing a regional maritime emission control area, India- US maritime cooperation, and the South China Sea arbitration award are analysed in the context of Blue Economy.

The last section highlights the role of maritime governance and the importance of capacity building for Blue Economy. Strengthening of ocean governance in the 'High Seas', developing a 'software' for the Blue Economy, the role of citizens in India's maritime resurgence, and the need for generating awareness, education and financing for promoting the Blue Economy are presented.

The volume also offers an easy access to important documents which are relevant to the development of the Blue Economy and presents them chronologically in the Appendix as further reading.

We hope that the volume wets the appetite of the layman as well as the informed reader. It is our sincere endeavour to promote the adoption of the Blue Economy around the world and to contribute to the development of the rapidly growing discourse on Blue Economy.

– Vijay Sakhuja

– Kapil Narula

Concept

Blue Economy –The Concept

The use of the oceans has diversified from classic medium of transport to that as a wellspring for resources. The economic richness of the oceans is represented by the variety of living resources (fish and marine vegetation which provide human protein and feed for other species), material goods (hydrocarbons, minerals, and sand & gravel), services (shipping, ports, shipbuilding, fishing, tourism), and renewables (wind, wave, tidal, thermal, biomass). These have acted as catalyst for the development of a number of industries both on land and at sea. Further, the seas and oceans have attracted humanity to the coastline who draw their employment and livelihoods from various activities.

In recent times, environment, ecology and sustainable use of the ocean-based resources have found reference in the maritime and marine discourse and in 2015, the global community announced its commitment to Sustainable Development Goals 2030 in which Goal 14 relates to sustainable development of the ocean resources. Significantly, Goal 14 is also linked to other SDG Goats such as SDG 1 (poverty), SDG 2 (food security), SDG 6 (water and sanitation), SDG 7 (energy), SDG 8 (economic growth), SDG 9 (infrastructure), SDG 10 (reduction of inequality), SDG 11 (cities and human settlements), SDG 12 (sustainable consumption and production), SDG 13 (on climate change), SDG 15 (biodiversity), and SDG 17 (means of implementation and partnerships).

Several states, particularly the maritime states, have endorsed the concept of Blue Economy which is currently resonating in the United Nations, multilateral institutions, and national policy articulations.

Economic Value of the Oceans

According to the United Nations, the commercial value of various activities in the world's oceans is estimated to be between US $3 trillion to US $6 trillion and is accrued from services and resources such as marine transport (90 per cent of global trade moves over the seas), global telecommunications (submarine cables carry 95 per cent of all digital data across the globe), source of food (fisheries and aquaculture feed 4.3 billion people with more than 15 per cent of annual consumption of animal protein), oil and gas (over 30 per cent is produced from offshore), marine tourism (5 per cent of the global gross domestic product (GDP) and 6 to 7 per cent of global employment), shore based commercial activity (13 of the world's to 20 megacities and over 40 per cent, or 3.1 billion, of the world population lives within 100 kilometers of the ocean or sea in about 150 coastal cities located along the coast and island nations). Besides, the oceans provide pharmaceuticals and sea vegetation as food, and emerging sources of energy such as tides, waves, currents, and offshore wind are being increasingly tapped to enhance energy security.

According to another estimate, the value of key ocean assets is conservatively estimated to be at least US $24 trillion with an annual value of goods and services of US $2.5 trillion. Further, the oceans are pegged at seventh position among the world's top 10 economies.

What is Blue Economy?

Gunter Pauli, an entrepreneur and an innovator, authored a book *The Blue Economy: 10 years – 100 innovations – 100 million jobs* aimed at stimulating entrepreneurship based on sustainability and health of the environment. He argued that humans should judiciously use the resources keeping in mind the social and environmental consequences, and any waste should be converted into a resource. Further, the focus should shift from identifying the problems to finding solutions.

In 2012, during the United Nations Conference on Sustainable Development (UNCSD) in Rio de Janeiro, (also called as 'Rio +20'), the concept of Green Economy for 'sustainable development and poverty eradication' was promoted, but the island states questioned the relevance and applicability of Green Economy to them and argued that 'the world's Oceans and Seas require more in-depth attention and coordinated action'. Soon thereafter, a number of UN led initiatives led by the UN Department of Economic and Social Affairs (DESA) expert group meeting on Oceans, Seas and Sustainable Development, the Global Ocean Commission, the

Global Partnership for Oceans and the UN five-year Action Agenda 2012-2016 provided the necessary impetus to the concept of Blue Economy. The UN also expanded the mandate of the 1982 United Nations Convention on the Law of the Sea (UNCLOS) and began to address sea spaces beyond national jurisdiction and called for an 'intergovernmental conference aimed at drafting a legally binding treaty to conserve marine life and govern the mostly lawless high seas beyond national jurisdiction'.

Blue Economy is currently resonating among a number of countries across the world and finding reference in the action plans for the sustainable development of resources, climate change and environment discourses, and national plans for enhancing wellbeing, and poverty alleviation among the people through job creation, have been endorsed.

Defining Blue Economy

Blue Economy is a combination of traditional sectors such as shipbuilding, shipping, ports and fisheries. Marine tourism or the marine leisure industry and cruise liner industry is another important sector of Blue Economy. Blue Economy also includes an assortment of new technology-oriented sectors that are capable of supporting advanced marine bio-prospecting through exploration and study of the marine ecosystems, marine organisms and animals, plants, algae and vegetation and multi-species aquaculture. These are important ingredients for a number of products which are essential as proteins in the form of food and feed, pharmaceuticals, cosmetics and other products. Besides, technologies capable of generating energy through tidal wave and sea based wind farms are already in operation. Another important facet of the development of Blue Economy is human resource who could also be entrepreneurs, start-ups, and the role of MSMEs cannot be underestimated.

At the core of the Blue Economy lies the idea of optimization of natural marine resources within ecological limits' and 'de-coupling of socio-economic development from environmental degradation'. The Blue Economy involves a number of interdependent sectors, which harness the wealth of the seas for economic growth through sustainable use.

A number of definitions have been attached to Blue Economy and it may be defined as follows:

The Blue Economy is envisaged as the integration of water based economy including inland water body & ocean economy development with the principles of social inclusion, environmental sustainability and innovative, dynamic business models.

Blue Economy and Security

There is a symbiotic relationship between Blue Economy and security. The 1982 UNCLOS III establishes a comprehensive framework for the regulation and management of the ocean space and addresses a broad spectrum of issues relating to regulation of navigation, marine protection, scientific research and seabed mining. Coastal states have accrued expansive sea spaces, designated as Exclusive Economic Zone (EEZ) under the UNCLOS III, and these have the promise of enormous living and non-living sea wealth. This sea space also provides for sovereign ownership for commercial activity in the EEZ, be it to catch fish, recover any oil and gas in the area, or mine or extract other marine resources. Although the UNCLOS III regime may have brought about 'order at sea' in terms of management of the sea spaces and resources, it has generated tensions among states, particularly when states declare national jurisdiction over deputed sea spaces, begin to exercise sovereignty and exploit resources.

In order to tackle many of these challenges, maritime law enforcement agencies such as the coast guards and marine police have been mandated to ensure safety and security of economic assets and activities such as offshore oil platforms, protection of marine wealth, prevent illegal fishing, and help uphold national environmental regulations thereby ensuring sustainable economic, livelihoods of coastal populations as also uphold national commitments to international agreements and initiatives such as the SDG 2030.

India is poised to emerge as a major maritime power and has located the Blue Economy high on its agenda for economic growth. The overarching objective is to develop Blue Economy through a robust regulatory framework which contributes to sustainable use of existing natural resources. The Indian government encourages proactive and facilitative governance which supports job creation, encourages innovation, and provides opportunities for knowledge-based businesses in key maritime sectors. In essence, a clear national vision and a road map for 'blue revolution growth' are clearly visible. It can be successfully fulfilled by a variety of stakeholders, businesses, industries, institutions, academia with the government providing the requisite 'software' of Blue Economy.

Delivering on the Promises of Sustainable Development Goal 14 for Oceans

193 countries of the world unanimously adopted the 2030 agenda for sustainable development in the form of 17 indivisible Sustainable Development Goals (SDGs) in September 2015. These goals which succeeded the Millennium Development Goals (MDGs) from 01 January 2016 will drive the world development agenda for the next 15 years.

The first review of the progress in achieving SDGs was undertaken at the High-Level Political Forum (HLPF) from 11-20 July 2016, at UN headquarters in New York. The meeting was considered important as the forum is the central platform for the follow up and review of SDGs. The forum which concluded with a ministerial declaration helped to identify the existing gaps in the SDG framework and its implementation and set the benchmark for progress on future monitoring efforts. 22 countries presented the results and experiences from voluntary national reviews (VNRs) of the SDGs to enable other members to learn from national actions and the accompanying implementation challenges.

The HLPF provided an opportunity for countries to demonstrate their preparedness in implementing the SDGs. This opportunity was exploited by countries like China, Germany, Philippines, Mexico and even smaller states like Togo, Morocco, Egypt and Uganda which presented VNR to showcase their progress in attaining the SDGs. However, India missed a golden opportunity to demonstrate its seriousness in pursuing the SDGs. Nevertheless, Mr. Arvind Panagariya, Vice-Chairperson of NITI Aayog, who represented India as a lead discussant in one of the sessions of the VNR did comment that while growth is a very important component, "there is a clear interplay between national development objectives and the SDGs". It may therefore be inferred that the SDG framework will hopefully be integrated in the development planning process in India.

Goal 14 for the oceans viz. "Conserve and sustainably use the oceans, seas and marine resources for sustainable development" has seven targets and three sub-targets. Various aspects such as limiting marine pollution, protecting biodiversity, marine habitat and ecosystems, minimizing and addressing the impacts of ocean acidification, regulating fishing and restoring ocean health are covered under these targets. The targets are tracked using 10 indicators which were developed by the interagency and expert group (IAEG) on SDG indicators for accurately measuring and monitoring the progress of various targets under the 17 SDGs. These set of indicators are an important component for reviewing the progress in achieving the SDGs at the global level and were adopted along with a global indicator framework by the 47th session of the United Nations Statistical Commission in March 2016 for closely monitoring the SDGs. A complete list of the targets of goal 14 and specific indicators is placed at Appendix.

Preliminary reports by the UN on meeting the targets of goal 14 indicate that there have been mixed results. The first indicator for measuring target 14.4 (which aims to restore fish stocks for maximising their yield) is the level of biologically sustainable fishing. Fig. 1 shows the share of fish stocks within biologically sustainable level. This indicator declined from 90 per cent in 1974 to 69 per cent in 2013 and the downward trend is clearly evident.

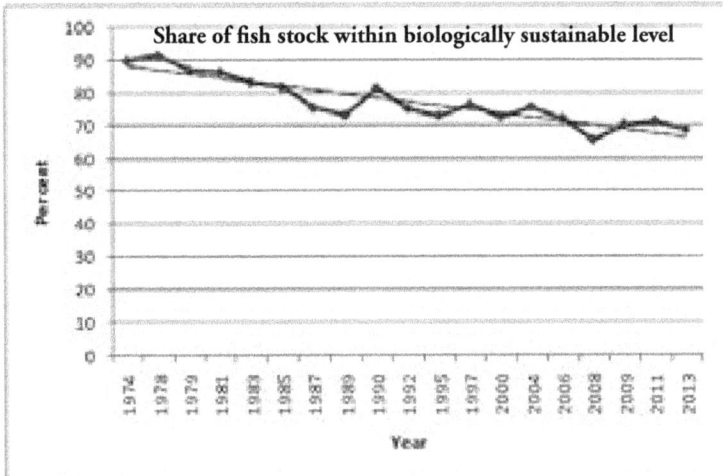

Fig. 1. Proportion of fish stocks within biologically sustainable limits

The second indicator measures the coverage of protected areas in relation to marine areas for different countries (target 14.5). It was heartening to note that the coverage of coastal and marine areas under protection has increased fourfold since 2000. In 2014, 8.4 per cent of the marine environment in the SEZ and 0.25 per cent of the marine environment beyond national jurisdiction were protected as against 1.9 per cent of the total area in 2000. In addition, the share of marine key biodiversity areas that were completely covered by protected areas increased from 15 per cent to 19 per cent from 2000 to 2016.

Measuring and monitoring the progress on SDG is vital and indicators play a very important role in this process, as what cannot be measured cannot be improved. In this context, there are certain limitations for SDG 14. The global website for monitoring SDGs has data on only two out of the existing ten indicators for goal 14 which hints at the difficulty and lack of preparedness to measure and monitor the indicators.

The second issue is the appropriateness of the indicator for measuring the relevant target and the amiability of the selected indicator to measurement. A case in point is the measurement of pollutants in sea in pursuit of the target 14.1 viz. 'significantly reducing marine pollution of all kinds'. The selected indicator is 'Nitrogen use efficiency composite indicator', a value which is complicated to compute as well as monitor.

The third aspect in the national context is the role and responsibility of different agencies in achieving the SDGs. Effectiveness and mechanisms of governance both at federal and state level are a major factor in the success of implementation of SDGs. In the specific case of India, the Niti Aayog is the nodal governmental agency for coordinating SDG implementation. In addition, the Ministry of Statistics and Programme Implementation (MoSPI) is the coordinating agency for tracking and reporting of data. The Ministry of Earth Sciences is the nodal ministry for Goal 14 which is being implemented under the centrally sponsored scheme of 'conservation of natural resources and ecosystems'. There are two related interventions: National plan for conservation of aquatic ecosystem and the 'Sagarmala' project. The department of animal husbandry, dairying and fisheries and the Ministry of Environment, Forests and Climate Change (MoEF&CC) are the other concerned agencies which are implementing this goal. However, it is still not clear, who will set up the monitoring stations and undertake collection, recording, processing and updation of data at the level of the states, near the respective coastlines and beyond the territorial waters.

The last issue is the additional effort, financial resources and human capital which have to be allocated out of the existing resources for monitoring the SDGs and associated efforts. The role of international organizations and cooperation amongst specialised ocean agencies is the key to overcoming these obstacles. All coastal states do not have adequate resources for collecting data as well as the capacity to undertake oceanographic observations and data processing. Hence apart from financial assistance, technical as well as human assistance needs to be provided to various states. Coordination, coherence and integration of effort is also essential.

While the 17 SDGs are indivisible and equally important, some of the SDGs such as Goal 14 for oceans are bound to be neglected due to lack of perceived importance of the goal as compared to other relevant social and economic goals. This tendency needs to be guarded against and governments must involve the civil society, specialised agencies and technical institutions to leverage their expertise for the monitoring of SDGs. While the deadline of 2030 may be far, the impetus attained in the initial stages in pursuing and measuring these goals is vital for the success of the 2030 agenda for sustainable development. Therefore, sustained and focused efforts are critical.

Marine Spatial Planning: Key to Blue Economy

The thrust towards economic and sustainable management of ocean spaces is fast gaining momentum across the globe. Also, States are placing biodiversity, conservation of the oceans, and coastal areas high on the agenda, particularly to support the Sustainable Development Goals 2030. Further, amidst the euphoria of developing Blue Economy, policy makers, planners, industry stakeholders, and the scientific community have invested enormous political, diplomatic, scientific, fiscal and technological capital in marine spatial planning. This is considered critical for the development and the growth of Blue Economy through optimal utilization of resource in a responsible and sustainable manner.

The United Nations Educational, Scientific and Cultural Organization (UNESCO) defines marine spatial planning as a "public process of analyzing and allocating the spatial and temporal distribution of human activities in marine areas to achieve ecological, economic, and social objectives that usually have been specified through a political process. Characteristics of marine spatial planning include ecosystem-based, area-based, integrated, adaptive, strategic and participatory". It further notes that marine spatial planning is "not an end in itself, but a practical way to create and establish a more rational use of marine space and the interactions among its uses, to balance demands for development with the need to protect the environment, and to deliver social and economic outcomes in an open and planned way".

Simply put, marine spatial planning can be understood as a process in which information relating to various aspects of the oceans such as engaging different users of the marine spaces and finding out where uses in the ocean and coastal zone occur, mapping these out and making it available for use by a number of stakeholders. This methodical approach helps conceptualize new marine projects keeping in mind the existing infrastructure and services related to the oceans which are collated and readily available to assess each project.

The concept of marine spatial planning has its genesis in ocean zoning in which it served as a tool for developing marine protected areas (MPAs) and today its usage is being acknowledged in marine bioregional planning concepts for an ecosystem-based marine spatial management.

In the coming decades, human activities in many areas of the ocean will increase significantly and new technologies would be developed to harness the wealth contained therein. A number of traditional uses of the oceans and seas such as transportation, fisheries, exploitation of living and non-living resources, sand and gravel mining, and marine tourism and leisure will continue to grow in size and economic value. There will be additional stresses on the oceans due to deep ocean human activity, overfishing resulting in diminished stocks; climate induced changes resulting in species distributions and habitats and ocean acidification will challenge the survival of many species. There will also be growing public concern over the health of the ocean which will demand significant investments in marine conservation. It is not beyond the realm of imagination that conflicting interests among conservationists and exploiters will increase. In essence, competing interests among various stakeholders would have to be addressed to harness the oceans and seas in a sustainable manner. The aim would be to achieve a balance in favour of clean, safe, healthy, productive and biologically diverse oceans. This will surely bring several benefits to the humankind as also to the marine environment as hitherto. Thus an environmental and ecologically based marine spatial planning of human activities would be critical for balancing various activities in the marine world so that they can co-exist and the impact of different activities on each other and the cumulative effects on the environment as a whole are addressed and managed in a balanced way.

In this context, there will be several benefits that will accrue to the industry which will help them to identify and developing various commercial activities based on data on marine ecosystems and their uses; understand regulatory and processes for obtaining permission, reducing legal impediments, uphold judicious management of resources as also address risks to prevent insecurity among the investors thereby helping in optimal utilization of both public and private funds.

A number of countries have embarked on marine spatial planning process and they are addressing various challenges in planning as also those that can be predicted. These include initiatives such evaluating new offshore renewable energy installations (sea based windmills, solar installations and wave energy harnessers), aquaculture farms, desalination plants, marine recreation to avoid excessive human footprints, and identifying new marine protected areas which serve as the fountainhead of marine and aquatic life.

Marine spatial planning is a continuous process and requires whole of government and people centric approach where the stakeholders have to plan the implementation and to undertake monitoring and evaluation. They will also have to develop alternatives to bring about changes in ongoing activities yet sustaining the original activity. A multinational and multi-industry leadership alliance pivoting on 'Corporate Ocean Responsibility' needs to be conceptualized wherein the industry participation in marine-related programme contributes to social development.

Marine Resources

Sustainable Exploitation of Marine Fish in India

There are nearly 200,000 identified species in the oceans, but their actual numbers may be in millions. Further, more than 3 billion people depend on the oceans as their primary supplement of protein and fish is an important source. The sector employs (directly or indirectly) over 200 million people across the globe. However, indiscriminate human activities, loss of coastal habitats, marine pollution and over exploitation are resulting in depleted fisheries and can potentially impact on the supply of marine based proteins.

According to WWF Global, the global fishing fleet is 2-3 times higher than what the oceans can sustainably support. The FAO Fisheries Department under the United Nations has noted with concern that nearly 53 per cent of the world's fisheries are fully exploited, and 32 per cent are overexploited, depleted, or recovering from depletion. Also, several important commercial fish populations have declined to the point where their survival is threatened.

As far as India is concerned, it ranks sixth in marine capture fish production (4.2 per cent of total) and third (4.8 per cent of total) in farmed aquaculture production. The Indian Ministry of Agriculture data shows that there has been a gradual increase in India's share in production of fish worldwide. Currently, marine fishermen population in India is estimated at 4.0 million and only 25 per cent are active fishermen. Of the total marine fish production, 75 per cent comes from the mechanized sector, 23 per cent from motorized sector and 2 per cent from artisanal sector. The government acknowledges the fact that "marine fish resources are not inexhaustible, and uncontrolled harvests will lead to depletion of resources, as experienced in many cases."

For instance, in the state of Goa there has been decline in fish catch particularly mackerel, which is a significant source of marine protein for generations, and prawns, one of the fastest selling sea food, has decreased. A leading marine scientists has suggested that Goa may be on the verge of a fish famine and observed that natural causes such as climate change, decreased dissolved oxygen (in the seas), man-made activities such as overfishing and marine pollutants, has been responsible for decline fish produce by the state.

Likewise, the popular Hilsa fish is in sharp decline across Asia due to over fishing and high pollution in the rivers. Some states have promulgated ban on fishing at the height of the breeding season (October-November). However, Bangladesh has witnessed increase in Hilsa capture due to robust fish management plans. For instance, in 2014,the government announced 11-day ban on fishing in all rivers, estuary and seas which was prolonged to 15 days in 2015. In 2016, the ban was for 22 days and according to reports "Catching, selling, transportation, storage and exchange of Hilsa fish" was banned across Bangladesh and enforced in a 7,000 square kilometer area designated as the breeding zone.

In the Palk Bay, South India, overexploitation of fish has been the feature and resulted from excessive use of mechanized trawlers that not only caused environmental damage and loss fish catch but resulted in political tensions between India and Sri Lanka. Likewise, there are issues of overexploitation from the Gujrat coast where Indian and Pakistani fishermen compete for fish capture. As far as India is concerned, the declining catch is due to excess number of fishing vessel i.e. in 2011, there were 35,150 fishing vessels which have been termed as "overcapacity with larger fishing fleets competing for the limited fisheries resource".

There are also issues of illegal and overexploitation of fish by Indian fishermen crossing over from adjoining states. These have been referred to as 'Rogue Fishermen' who cross over from Karnataka and Maharashtra into Goa's waters and fish using dragnets and "scooping out tons of fish from the bottom of the sea, including young off-springs and even eggs, thus, killing the chances of any replenishment of livestock". This prompted State government of Goa to start thinking about deploying patrol vessel as a "signal to such robbers" amid reports of 27 boats having been caught over the last three years.

At the global level, there is also ample evidence that fish from the high seas which account for 42 per cent of the oceans are being overexploited. Spain, China and Japan have been accused of disproportionate fishing in the high seas. In the case of China, its annual catch in the seas was 13 million tons as against the allowed volume set between 8 million to 9 million tons. According to China's Ministry of Agriculture, fishery resources are severely depleted in East China Sea and similar conditions prevail in the Yellow Sea and the Bohai Sea. There are now calls to impose ban for 10 years in the Yangtze River which is regarded as a cradle of China's freshwater fisheries and a valuable reserve of aquatic biodiversity.

While it is fair to acknowledge the adversarial impact of overexploitation of fishery resources from the sea, equally important is the need to develop sophisticated fisheries management plans aimed at conservation of fisheries resources keeping in mind the social and economic factors that are likely to override in some cases. In this context,sustainable exploitation of marine living resources is an important facet of development of Blue Economy. This aspect has also been reinforced by the universally accepted Sustainable Development Goals 2030 in which Goal 14 calls for conserving and sustainably using the oceans, seas and marine resources.

Six Steps to Combatting IUU Fishing

The 2014 Global Ocean Commission Report from Decline to Recovery: A Rescue Package for the Global Ocean has likened the high seas to a 'failed State' where 'lawlessness verging on anarchy' prevails and it is free for 'plunder and neglect'. Eighteen months after the report was released, the authors have concluded that although threats to the health of the oceans persist, there have been tangible changes and the global community is willing to work to reduce the vulnerability of the seas.

One of the important issues of concern for the Global Ocean Commission was Illegal, Unreported and Unregulated (IUU) fishing, also referred as 'pirate fishing'. The IUU fishing involves operations that do not adhere to national or international laws, unlicensed fishing operations, illegal transshipments or transfers at sea of fish catch to other vessels, catching protected species, and not adhering to the regulations in force announced by the local and relevant regional fishery management organization (RFMO).

IUU fishing affects the sustainability of fish stocks. According to the Food and Agriculture Organization (FAO) of the United Nations, nearly 50 per cent of marine fish stocks are fully exploited, 15-18 per cent is over exploited, and 10 per cent are already depleted. Further, the annual global fish catch in 2010 was about 109 million metric tons, but official reports submitted by more than 200 countries and territories totaled 77 million which means that 32 million metric tons of fish goes unreported.

The Global Ocean Commission listed six steps to combat and end IUU fishing to promote transparency and institute accountability of the fishing industry. First, it called for mandatory requirements of IMO (International Maritime Organization) numbers and tracking arrangements similar to those on merchant ships for all vessels engaged in fishing in the high seas. It is mandatory for all merchant vessels above 300 tons to install the Automatic Identification System (AIS), which helps in tracking vessels at sea. There are reports of fishing vessels turning off the AIS devices to prevent detection and tracking, and continue IUU fishing operations, which according to the Commission is a worrying trend.

Second, the Commission was concerned about 'at-sea transshipment' of fish catch. Fishing vessels are known to operate for long periods and transfer the catch to other vessels thereby successfully circumventing coastal and port State control regimes. These vessels are difficult to detect because they generally operate in disputed waters or where the law enforcement is weak. Further, the maritime enforcement agencies seldom patrol outside their Exclusive Economic Zones (EEZ) and IUU fishers pursue their business undetected with total impunity.

Third, the Commission is hoping that all port States become Party to the FAO Agreement on Port State Measures to Prevent, Deter and Eliminate IUU Fishing (PSMA). By January 2016, 19 States had signed the PSMA and the Commission was hopeful that other States would support the effort to ensure its entry into force by July 2016.

Fourth, the Commission was of the view that real-time information sharing and global data on high seas fishing vessels and their activities is critical to deter IUU fishing as also to help trace defaulting vessels. This requires robust maritime domain awareness, which is technology intensive. In the Indian Ocean, the Information Management and Analysis Centre (IMAC) in India and the Singapore-based Information Fusion Centre (IFC) established at Changi Command and Control Centre (CC2C), serve as effective MDA hubs. Currently, these are meant for strengthening maritime and coastal security against unusual or suspicious movements and activities at sea and can be used for monitoring of IUU fishing activity.

Fifth, the consumers of seafood have an important role to play in preventing, deterring, and eliminating IUU fishing. At the State level, vessels suspected of IUU fishing operations can be prevented to land fish brought to port for trade. Further, fish traceability is an effective mechanism to curb IUU fishing. For instance, the US National Ocean Council Committee to Combat Illegal, Unreported and Unregulated Fishing and Seafood Fraud has proposed a seafood traceability system that will collect data about harvest, landing, and chain of custody of fish and fish products brought into the United States and if the catch is found suspicious, list it as seafood fraud.

Sixth, the civil society organizations can play an important role as watchdogs and compliment international, regional and State efforts to curb IUU fishing. It is a well-known fact that laws and regulations are difficult to enforce in international waters. Also, labour onboard such vessels are largely undocumented who work in inhumane conditions. Some of these are refugees or migrants who take risks for livelihood and constantly fear for their safety and security. For instance, European Union Commissioner for Fisheries, Maritime Affairs and Environment has been asked to approach Thailand to institute reforms in its fishing industry to ensure that its exports are not from IUU fishing, and human rights of the fishermen were upheld.

It is true that sea is an important source of protein for nearly 4.3 billion people but IUU fishing adversely affect the ecological, economic and social conditions of countries. Further, IUU fishing is an important issue of concern under the ten targets contained in Sustainable Development Goal (SDG) 14. It therefore becomes incumbent on the States to understand the impact of IUU fishing on the marine ecosystem and food supply chain both for life at sea and humanity ashore. This can be achieved by developing effective measures to enhance transparency, institute accountability, and develop technological capability to monitor IUU fishing in international waters.

India Endeavours to Tap into Ocean Energy

Oceans occupy more than 70 per cent of the earth's surface and are an unlimited source of renewable energy. It is estimated that ocean energy can provide upto 1,000,000 EJ of renewable energy per year; second only to solar energy which has a resource availability of 3,900,000 EJ per year. However, out of this annual energy flow, only a small fraction can be harnessed and the technical potential of ocean energy is estimated at 3,240- 10,500 EJ per year, while that for solar energy is 62,000-280,000 EJ per year. To put these numbers in perspective the total energy consumed in the entire world in 2015 was approximately 500 EJ. It is therefore evident that oceans are an inexhaustible source of energy.

India has three distinct energy challenges: to meet it's ever increasing energy demand, to lower GHG emissions, and to provide clean energy at low cost. These three seemingly contradicting end goals are to be met by 2030 in order to meet the Sustainable Development Goal 7 (SDG 7) on energy viz. 'Ensure access to affordable, reliable, sustainable and modern energy for all'.

Realizing the potential of ocean energy and its relevance for India, the Union Cabinet gave its approval for India to become a member country of the Ocean Energy Systems (OES) by signing the Implementing Agreement (IA) on 13 Jan 2016. The OES 2 Energy Technology Initiative is an intergovernmental collaboration between countries which operate under the aegis of International Energy Agency (IEA) and currently has 23 member countries including China, US, UK and other EU countries. This process of induction was formally completed on 27 April 2016 when India joined the Technology Collaboration Programme of the OES. The Earth System Science Organisation at the National Institute of Ocean Technology (ESSO-NIOT) under the Ministry of Earth Sciences is the nodal agency which will lead the Indian initiatives. Ocean energy is primarily of six different types:

(a) Wave energy: Based on wind-wave interaction.

(b) Tidal energy: Based on rise and fall of water level due to gravitational pull of sun and the moon.

(c) Tidal stream: Water flow in channels located on coast due to tidal effects.

(d) Ocean Thermal Energy Conversion (OTEC): Due to differential in temperature between different depths in the ocean.

(e) Salinity gradients: Due to difference in osmotic pressure between fresh water and salty water found in the region where the river meets the sea.

(f) Ocean currents: Which are wind-driven or based on thermohaline circulation.

In addition, there are other potential sources of oceanic energy such as extraction of biofuel from seaweed algae and geothermal energy from submarine vents, but these technologies are relatively unproven.

While tidal energy is a well-established technology and a 240 MW tidal plant has been operating since 1966 at La Rance in France. The largest and the latest addition to tidal energy is the deployment of 254 MW plant at Sihwa Lake, South Korea in 2011. As there has to be a minimum difference of 7 mts between the low and the high tide, there are limited regions in the world which are suited for setting up tidal plants. In India, the total identified potential of tidal energy is about 9,000 MW which is distributed in three regions: Gulf of Cambay (7000 MW), Gulf of Kutch (1200 MW) and the Ganges Delta in 3 the Sunderbans (100 MW). A 3.65 MW plant is functional in the Sunderbans and a 50MW plant is planned in the Gulf of Khambhat and Kutch. The upfront investment cost for the plant is around 4,500-5,000 US $/KW and with a lifetime of 40 years, the levelised cost of electricity (LCOE) is around 17-25 cents/kWh. While this LCOE makes tidal energy as one of the cheapest form of ocean energy, the cost is still higher than electricity generated from fossil fuels as well as clean energy sources such as wind and solar, which is a big barrier for adoption of the technology.

Wave energy is most potent in latitudes between 30-60 degrees and has reached full scale prototype demonstration. There are various existing technologies such as wave attenuators, point absorbers, oscillating waves surge converters, oscillating water column, overtopping devices etc. which are deployed throughout the world. The investment cost is relatively steep and ranges from 6,200-16,000 US $/KW, and the technologies have a lifetime of approximately 20 years. The total installed capacity of wave energy generators was 12 MW in 2014.

Tidal stream has also been deployed in single array and consists of horizontal axis turbines which are similar to wind turbines as well as vertical axis/cross flow devices which are installed underwater. These require a minimum flow of 1.5-2 m/s of water and require an investment of 5,400-14,300 US $/KW. The total installed capacity for tidal stream in 2014 was around 14 MW.

OTEC plants are most suitable for deployment in 0-35 degree latitudes as a temperature differential of 22-degree C is required for its operation. This is available in tropical waters where the surface temperature can go upward of 26 degree and cold water at 4-8-degree C can be extracted from depths of 800-1000 m. OTEC plants having a capacity of 10-100 KW have been deployed in India, US, and Japan. This technology is also preferred for deployment close to islands as it produces fresh water as a byproduct which can be used for drinking. NIOT had deployed an OTEC closed cycle plant of size 1 MW on a floating platform, 'Sagar Shakti' in 2000 off the coast of Tuticorin which was the largest plant ever tested at that time. The Indian Navy is also exploring setting up a 20 MW OTEC plant off the coast of Andaman & Nicobar Islands, pre-feasibility study for which have already been conducted by DCNS, France.

The other two technologies based on harnessing salinity gradients and ocean currents are relatively at an early stage of development. Although there are lab scale models, there is no scaled prototype for commercial generation of electricity from these technologies and it is anticipated that these will have to be substantially developed before deployment at sea.

There are many challenges such as the harsh corrosive environment of the sea, technological limitations such as daily and seasonal variability of waves and currents, requirement of power conditioning and output smoothing due to a power cycle of the order of seconds and low energy density of ocean energy. Other infrastructural issues such as power evacuation using submersible electricity carrying cables, distance of the plant from the shore, provisioning of offshore platform for plant installation also increases the overall cost of electricity generation.

Ocean energy is abundant, is emission free and forms a key component of the 'Blue Economy'. India's efforts to advance research, development and demonstration of ocean energy technologies in collaboration with the OES is laudable and it is likely that India will now have access to advanced technologies. Personnel will additionally have the opportunity to partner with other leading agencies and to join R&D teams across the world to develop cutting edge solutions to overcome the existing challenges and limitations. India will also benefit from being a part of developing test protocols and testing of Indian prototypes can now be undertaken based on international standards. What now remain to be seen is how the technology is scaled up and how fast the costs are brought down so that ocean energy can become a significant part of the global energy mix.

Marine Infrastructure and Transport

Green Ports: Going beyond Renewable Energy Generation

Maritime India Summit (MIS) 2016 which is an endeavour of the Government of India to promote growth of the maritime sector in the country was held in Mumbai from 14-16 April 2016. Various initiatives such as port modernization, new port development, inland waterways, hinterland connectivity & multimodal logistics, international & coastal shipping, ship building, ship repair & ship recycling, port led industrialisation, cruise shipping & lighthouse tourism and green initiatives in ports are being showcased to attract investors and to explore the potential business opportunities in the maritime sector.

While promoting the maritime sector, the Ministry of Shipping also launched 'Project Green Ports' in January 2016 and integrated twelve 'Green Ports Initiatives' with the existing 'Swachh Bharat Abhiyaan'. The Green Port Initiatives include aspects such as preparation and planning for monitoring environmental pollution, acquiring pollution monitoring equipment, acquiring dust suppression system, setting up of sewage/waste water treatment plants/ garbage disposal plant, setting up projects for energy generation from renewable energy sources, completion of shortfalls of Oil Spill Response (OSR) facilities (Tier-1), prohibition of disposal of almost all kind of garbage at sea and improving the quality of harbour wastes.

As a part of the above drive, green initiatives in ports are also being encouraged as a sunrise segment in MIS 2016 in order to ensure environmentally benign operations and sustainable development of ports. 135 MW of solar power projects across eight major ports and 50 MW of wind energy projects across three major ports are planned to be installed by 2020. The shipping ministry has also introduced an incentive scheme to promote the use of green energy at major ports and will share up to 50 per cent of the total cost for waste water treatment projects and to promote the use of bio-diesel. As a part of these incentives, each port will be given a financial grant up to Rs 25 crore (US$ 4 Million) for undertaking these projects. Certain measures for monitoring pollution of marine environment and issue of anti-fouling certificate to Indian ships above 400 Gross Tons (GT) has also been proposed. While it is a good start, green port initiatives need to move beyond the physical generation of renewable energy in port premises and the principles of environmental sustainability have to be enshrined in the planning, development and operation of ports.

Green ports have a small ecological footprint. Such ports are sustainable and balance the economic, environmental and social dimensions of development. The design and construction of these ports promote low energy operations, maximize resource efficiency, increase productivity and activities undertaken at these ports have minimal environmental impact. Green ports extend the above concepts to all port users including maritime transport and multimodal transportation which are used for hinterland connectivity. These ports are a key component of 'Blue Economy' and are commercially attractive for shipping due to the environmental benefits they create, balancing the investments and cash flows. Green ports lay emphasis on spatial planning including its surrounding areas, are highly networked and use integrated information and decision support systems for planning and execution of the logistics chain. These ports maintain stringent environmental standards for limiting water, land and air pollution and are adaptive as they include climate change mitigation and adaptation strategies. Activities undertaken at green ports can be divided into two categories: those undertaken by ships berthing in the ports and those undertaken by port administration for providing port services. Both of these are driven by green policies and incentives and green technologies become enablers for green ports. Major actors in green ports include ship owners, ship operators, marine fuel suppliers, shipyards, port terminal operators, classification societies and contractors providing utility services in the ports.

A green port utilizes renewable energy and has net zero energy buildings. However, every port jurisdiction may not be endowed with renewable energy sources such as solar irradiation and wind energy. Additionally, there may be constraints on the area available for installation of solar panels and issues of intermittency of renewable energy. Hence Indian green ports must look beyond physically setting up RE facilities inside the port areas and could be mandated to buy 'virtual green energy' in the form of 'Renewable Energy

Certificates' (RECs), as a fixed share of the total consumption of electricity. Additionally, Power Purchase Agreements (PPA) must be made with RE generators for a 3-contracted amount of power using the provisions of 'Open Access' of electricity, which enables any consumer to procure power from any producer of energy across India, irrespective of the place of generation or consumption. This electricity can be then extended to the ships while they are berthed in a port. This will lower emissions of SOx, NOx and Particulate Matter (PM) when ships are berthed alongside and would improve the air quality inside the port while building a green image.

Port administrators need to involve various stakeholders in discussion and should reach necessary agreements regarding the provisioning of port services by establishing the demand for energy services and by building the necessary, logistics chains and infrastructure for delivery of these services. Port design and planning also plays a very important role in ensuring port efficiency and there should be optimal use of space by building multi user and networked terminals. Transport planning for smooth movement of ships when entering and leaving the port will minimize the turnaround time and will lead to improvement in port productivity while lowering the environmental impact while the ship is in the port premises. Waste minimization as well as treatment of water (including ballast water) is to be specially emphasized and habitat management needs to be addressed so as to cause minimal impact to marine organisms.

Port governance and port management plays an important role in ensuring green ports and incentives such as reduction in port charges for environment friendly ships, as extended by other ports in the world such as Rotterdam and Hamburg will go a long way to promote green ports in India. San Diego, Singapore, Gothenburg, Vancouver and Hong Kong and examples of ports which are adopting green initiatives on similar lines.

Green Ports play an important role in the growth of India's maritime sector. This concept therefore needs to move from the fringes to the center of port operations and needs to be integrated in the planning process to ensure sustainable development of the Indian maritime sector.

Indian Marine Leisure Industry gets a Boost

The Maritime India Summit 2016 in Mumbai was the first ever large scale global maritime event hosted by India. It was also an opportune moment for the Indian Prime Minister to announce his vision of a 'maritime India' built around robust infrastructure to complement the hinterland development plans. The thrust of his speech was on 'leveraging the long coastline and natural maritime advantages' and invigorating the ocean economy through the Sagarmala project, which focuses on port-led development integrated with special economic zones, smart cities, industrial parks, logistics hubs and transport corridors. The Summit also served as a platform for investors to explore business opportunities in various maritime sectors.

One of the focus areas among these was the development of coastal and marine tourism along the 7,500 kilometers long coastline, which is dotted with pristine beaches, tranquil waterfronts and picturesque island territories. These are home to mangrove forests, nesting sites for sea turtles, sea grass beds, coral reefs and the adjacent waters are home to a variety of fish and mammals.

The renewed focus on marine tourism comes after decades of neglect by various governments; and Indian policy makers never envisioned marine tourism as an important part of the engine for the growth of national economy. The 1982 national policy on tourism did not succeed due to the closed nature of the Indian economy and restrictive licensing policy which denounced private and foreign participations. But the 2002 National Tourism Policy acknowledged tourism as an engine of economic growth and envisioned the sector as an economic multiplier under the framework of 'Government-led, private-sector driven and community-welfare oriented' and stressed the need to develop tourism in an environmentally sustainable environment manner.

Marine tourism industry has developed well along India's west coast – particularly around Goa along the Konkan belt, and in Kerala along the

Malabar Coast. Goa – referred to as 'Pearl of the Orient' – is a tourist paradise, and received 895 international charter flights in 2015. Similarly, Kerala, which is promoted as 'God's own country', attracts international tourists for its beaches, picturesque backwaters, canals, and lagoons, which are home to abundant marine life.

The Andaman and Nicobar Islands are an excellent tourism destination, but have been selectively opened for tourism due to environmental and security concerns. The islands are closer to popular tourist destinations such as Phuket in Thailand and Langkawi in Malaysia, but have remained closed to international cruise liners. Likewise, the Lakshadweep Islands offer the finest underwater marine life for scuba divers, but have remained insulated to tourism primarily due to security and controlled development reasons.

The Indian government initiative to boost marine tourism is laudable, and a number of agencies are engaged in promoting coastal and marine tourism through projects such as cruise shipping and lighthouse tourism. Cruise tourism is a neglected and overlooked industry, and Indian ports have not been a popular cruise destination among the cruise line industry. Significantly, most cruise liners bypass India, either to Southeast Asia or the Middle East; and in 2014, the sea arrivals constituted about 0.4 per cent of country's total foreign arrivals. The Indian government is conscious of infrastructure inadequacies and has a vision and plan for promotion of cruise tourism and increase sea arrivals to 1.2 million tourists by 2030-31. Cruise terminals are under development at Goa, Cochin, Mumbai and Chennai and these can potentially boost the domestic hospitality industry that is also developing infrastructure and services to support port city excursions and domestic tourism.

Another innovative marine tourism initiative by the government is lighthouse tourism. There are nearly 190 lighthouses along the Indian coast and the surrounding areas offer opportunities for development of hotels, resorts, viewing galleries, adventure sports, thematic restaurant and allied tourism facilities. The Directorate General of Lighthouses and Lightships have identified 78 lighthouses, and adjacent areas around 8 lighthouses are being developed for tourism.

There are at least three more marine tourism segments which merit attention. The first is marinas. The Kerala Tourism Development Corporation (KTDC) marina at Bolgatty Island in Kochi is of international standard, and can berth around 30 yachts. A number of foreign luxury yachts sailing through the Indian Ocean call at Kochi. Interestingly, it is the world's only marina with a golf course. Two new marinas are under development in Mumbai and Kolkata. Although the ownership and use of luxury yachts in India is not quite popular, and only about 500 registered leisure boats are berthed in existing port facilities, setting up marinas can be a major growth industry for building yachts, encourage ownership of luxury boats, revenue for ports and create jobs.

The second segment is water sports which is a major attraction for marine leisure and entertainment industry in India. Several facilities have sprung up along India's coast line and offer sailing, windsurfing, boating, water scooter rides, parasailing and jet skiing and their popularity is fast catching up. Most of the sea front tourist resorts and hotels too have now begun to offer these facilities. The National Institute of Water Sports (NIWS) at Goa offers training in Lifesaving Techniques and Powerboat Handling that is essential for running water sports facilities in India.

Third, India is also endowed with 14,500 kilometres of rivers, canals, backwaters, creeks and lakes of which 5600 kilometres is navigable by mechanized vessels. The government plans to develop 101 new waterways as national waterways and these have the potential of becoming tourism hubs. The Goa government has invited investments to develop its 250-kilometre inland waterways for connectivity, as also to attract tourism.

While marine tourism and recreation business is expected to be a growth industry in India and the government is committed to provide necessary policy and fiscal support and encouragement, many such infrastructure projects come under Coastal Regulation Zones. Given the fragile nature of the marine environment and the delicate marine biodiversity, any tourism and recreation development projects would have to be subjected to stringent environmental laws and regulations.

Blue Economy: Twinning Sagarmala and Smart Ports

Harbours and ports are critical for the sustained growth of Blue Economy. They link the hinterland industrial corridors/hubs and other special economic zones to international markets through various connectivity-transportation networks built around roads, rail and inland waterways.

India's coastline is dotted with 12 Major ports and 200 notified minor and intermediate Ports which facilitate nearly 90 per cent of the country's foreign trade by volume and 70 per cent by value. There has been a steady growth in the volume of traffic handled at these ports but only one Indian port figure in the top fifty container ports in the world.

In 2003, the Indian government announced the Sagarmala project with Rupees 1 Lakh crore investment to 'infuse new life into the neglected sectors of the maritime industry the inland waterways, coastal shipping and ship-building and repairs'. The project was put on hold due to political priorities of the next government but the current government has resurrected it and once again placed ports at the center of its ocean development plans and a number of initiatives have been announced.

The government plans to invest Rupees 12 lakh crore over the next ten years to develop 27 industrial clusters, and to improve connectivity with ports through new rail and road projects. Over 140 port projects connected with the 12 major ports have been earmarked for modernization under Sagarmala. These will be developed on the PPP model and a larger part of the cost will be borne by the ports themselves and the balance will be sourced from the private sector partners.

The Sagarmala can potentially result in a number of opportunities and the Indian shipping minister has indicated four strategic levers "(a) optimizing multi-modal transport to reduce the cost of domestic cargo; (b) minimizing the time and cost of export-import cargo logistics; (c) lowering costs for bulk industries by locating them closer to the coast; and (d) improving export competitiveness by locating discrete manufacturing clusters near ports." This is expected to result in annual savings in logistics cost of about Rupees 35,000 crore, boost India's merchandise exports to US $110 billion by 2025, and create nearly one crore new jobs, of which 40 lakh will be in the nature of direct employment.

The national strategy for ports pivots on a number of sectors including industrial development, manufacturing, marine tourism, shipping and river transportation. Further, port infrastructure would support offshore projects such as oil and gas development and sea based renewable energy programmes. While many of these projects are driven by commercial interests, they are to be environment friendly and sustainable.

At another level, information and communication technologies are critical for effective and efficient management of ports and the associated supply chains. These not only facilitate but enhance port capacity, ship and yard planning, optimize equipment and associated infrastructure utilization thereby improving overall performance of different terminals in the port facility.

In current times, major transformations are underway due to advanced levels of digitalization in all sectors of port operations and in witness is high degree of automation, use of smart sensors, global networks for data transfer, unmanned and remote controlled systems, and semi or fully autonomous operation by various sections of the port facility.

Significantly, growing digitalization, and the ever-expanding use of electronical data, has transformed the way modern ports operate. Majority of the operations in the ports use a variety of intelligent management systems which enable high efficiency thereby reducing human induced delays.

Another important outcome of the digitalization of the ports is the consolidation of physical and cyber which is referred to as Cyber-Physical System (CPS). These connect the physical world with the virtual world of information processing through software systems, communications technology, and sensors/actuators including embedded technologies.

For instance a ship is connected to a port through a number of onboard systems such as Electronic Chart Display Systems (ECDIS), Automatic

Identification system (AIS), the onboard Voyage Data Recorder (VDR) to record and store data of each voyage in electronic format and Global Maritime Distress and Safety System (GMDSS). Likewise, shipping agents are connected to the ship through digital cargo manifest, bill of lading and supply chain managers. As far as the ports are concerned, a number of stakeholders including port authorities, Stevedore service providers, repair and maintenance companies, customs agencies, health and quarantine authorities, are connected to the ship to provide various services. These form a unique ecosystem which can be termed as Maritime CPS.

Although the government remains committed to port-led development projects under Sagarmala, a weak cyber infrastructure to support the initiative could be the Achilles heel. These projects would require cyber-hardening to preclude disruption/destruction of operations. The ports would have to integrate cybersecurity in the Sagarmala initiative, institute stringent cybersecurity standards, conduct cyber vulnerability assessments, and prepare response plans. Simultaneously, ports would have to establish systems, protocols and processes to exchange cyber threat information, develop programmes to incentivize cybersecurity, and guarantee a functional information sharing network that continues to provide working environment for all the stakeholders.

Environmental Preservation

Paris Climate Deal: Implications for International Shipping

A historical climate deal was reached in Paris on 12 Dec 2015. The legally binding agreement which has been touted as differentiated, balanced, durable and ambitious aims to limit the increase in the global average temperature to "well below 2-degree C", above pre-industrial levels while "pursuing efforts to limit the temperature increase to 1.5-degree C". But what if any, are the implications of the agreement for international shipping? And, how can the maritime sector contribute to mitigating global GHG emissions?

International Shipping and CO2 Emissions

If international shipping was a country it would be the seventh largest GHG emitter in the world, in the year 2014. However, international shipping which contributes to 2-3 per cent and the aviation sector which contributes to approximately 2 per cent of the global carbon emissions were omitted from national commitments under the 1997 Kyoto Protocol. For the shipping sector, ships have different port of origin, destination port, intermediate ports of call, flag state of the ship (country where the ship is registered) and there are other actors in the industry such as private owners and operators of ships which have registered offices in all countries. Hence these sectors were excluded due to the complexity of accounting and appropriating emissions to countries. Nevertheless, due to environmental concerns on growing emissions the International Civil Aviation Organization (ICAO) and the International Maritime Organization (IMO) were mandated to frame and implement laws to control the emissions from these sectors.

Despite steps taken by the organizations, there was an 80 per cent increase in CO2 emissions from these sectors between 1990 and 2010, as compared to a growth of 40 per cent from other activities across the globe. Further, according to the third IMO GHG study, it is estimated that the

GHG emissions from international shipping are projected to grow to 6-14 per cent by 2050, an increase of 50-250 per cent from the business as usual (BAU) scenario due to increase in demand for seaborne transportation.

At the start of the negotiations the draft text of the Paris agreement had an explicit paragraph to control emissions from aviation and international shipping. However, during the course of the negotiations, the optional paragraph was omitted and these sectors are not included in the current climate deal. Therefore, the responsibility to control GHG emissions from the shipping sector continues to rest with the IMO and there would be no national effort to regulate emissions from international shipping.

IMO's Leadership Role

While the nature of activities and the non-homogeneity of the actors was an impediment in including international shipping in any country based GHG accounting framework, the sector, under the guidance of the IMO was able to successfully negotiate and adopt a model for controlling emissions. Three key agreements have been evolved by the IMO since 2010 under a sectoral framework, and these will continue to be implemented by the Marine Environment Protection Committee (MEPC) in a phased manner. These are:

(a) Adoption of NOx Emission Standards for engines.

(b) Reduction in sulfur content of fuel to contain SOx emissions.

(c) Mandatory mechanisms aimed at reducing GHG emissions from ships such as Energy Efficiency Design Index (EEDI) and implementation of Ship Energy Efficiency Management Plan (SEEMP).

Not undermining the efforts of the IMO to regulate emissions from international shipping within the overarching framework supported by UNFCCC, much more still remains to be done. An overall cap on emissions was resisted by the IMO in the run up to the Paris meeting on the plea that it would restrict the profitability of shipping and 3 would compromise on the industry's ability to meet the growing demand of the world's economy. However, the IMO expressed its solidarity with the global goal and has vowed to continue efforts to curb emissions from the sector.

An overall CO2 emissions cap for the sector has to be implemented equally across all countries for reductions of aggregate GHG emissions. Such an initiative has to be global and flag neutral and can be best delivered and implemented under the guidance and leadership of the IMO. Considering that the shipping sector continues to be 'a servant of the world economy' and that there are no overall caps which have been agreed in the Paris climate deal, the IMO is doing a decent job of driving the shipping industry on the path of lower CO2 emission intensity. The sectoral model which is applicable to all countries has triggered the growth of clean shipping and has the potential to reduce emissions of CO2 per tonne-km by 50 per cent by 2050. While an absolute cap may not be feasible as it is incident on the quantum of world trade, deeper emission intensity cuts which are in the range of 80-90 per cent have been suggested by 2050 if a 2-degree centigrade goal has to be met. An aggressive approach to meet this goal would also require that emissions from international shipping have to peak by 2020 and need to fall thereafter at a drastic pace. A CO2 neutral shipping industry by its own would be expensive to deliver and hence IMO must work towards offsetting these emissions by investing in carbon sinks in other sectors. Alternate options and other measures to reduce emissions were discussed in the 69th session of the MEPC meeting in April 2016.

Conclusion

While the global climate deal can be considered as a diplomatic success, it has left the maritime sector out of its ambit. This implies that the international shipping industry led by the IMO needs to demonstrate continued leadership for evolving binding agreements and for adopting targets which are consistent with the goal 1.5-2-degree C rise. The IMO is in a position to deliver a win-win arrangement as it can guide the sector to regulate itself while contributing to the global goal of attaining carbon neutrality. It can do this at a pace which is technologically feasible while maximizing profits and contributing to the growth of the world economy.

Fisheries and the Plastic Threat in Bay of Bengal

The 2016 Food and Agriculture Organisation (FAO) of the United Nations report on *State of World Fisheries and Aquaculture: Contributing to Food Security and Nutrition for All* notes that the world per capita fish supply reached a new high of 20 kilograms. Further, the global fish production for human consumption has grown from 93.4 million tons in 2014 to more than 146 million tonnes in 2016 which corresponds to 87 per cent of the world fish production utilized for direct human consumption, up from 85 per cent or 136 million tonnes in 2014.

Amid these promising trends in the fisheries sector, there are disturbing reports about the ever-increasing trash and flotsam at sea, bulk of which is plastic. The global production and consumption of plastics has continued to rise and it is estimated that nearly 269,000 tons of plastic corresponding to 5.25 trillion plastic particles is floating in the world's oceans. The leakage of plastics into the ocean is a consequence of inadequate and inefficient wastewater and solid waste collection and disposal techniques.

There are five gyres or slow rotating whirlpools located in the Indian Ocean, North and South Atlantic, and North and South Pacific. These experience high concentrations of floating micro-plastics and the Great Pacific Garbage Patch in the North Pacific (bound by coasts of China, Korea, Japan, Russia, Alaska and California) holds the highest concentration of plastic debris. Although sunlight and waves cause floating plastics to break into smaller particles, but they never completely disappear or biodegrade; instead, these small plastic disintegrate as micro-plastic (less than 4.75 mm), meso-plastic (4.75-200 mm) and macro-plastic (above 200 mm) and act as sponges for waterborne contaminants such as pesticides.

Perhaps what is most disturbing is the fact that plastic has been found inside fish and large mammals. For instance, in January 2016, 29 whales were found stranded on shores around the North Sea, an area that is too shallow for the marine wildlife. The internal examination of the whales revealed that their stomachs were full of plastic debris - a 13-meter-long fishing net; a 70-cm piece of plastic from a car; and other pieces of plastic of various sizes. Large size fish and other mammals inadvertently consume plastic as if they are eating fish and the digestive system does not permit excretion of the plastic. Consequently, the debris remains inside the body causing 'full stomachs' resulting in starvation.

The FAO report acknowledges the importance of fisheries as an important source of food and nutrition but it is also a source of contamination. The disintegrated plastic debris can potentially be ingested by the humans when they eat seafood resulting in a number of ailments including cancer. According to a study, nearly 80 per cent of Japanese anchovy caught in the Tokyo Bay had micro plastic waste inside their digestive systems. Similar waste has been found in the digestive systems of marine species - sea turtles, whales, clams and seabirds- in the US, Britain and Indonesia. Another study suggests that nearly 90 per cent of seabirds have ingested small plastic pieces.

The Bay of Bengal is rich in marine living resources and produces 6 million tons of fish which corresponds to nearly 4 per cent of the value of the global catch. It is an important source of food for nearly 400 million people in the region. The fishing industry employs 2.2 million fishers, 460,000 fishing trawlers, and offers livelihood for 4.5 million people.

Like any other large water body, the Bay of Bengal is littered with plastic and huge amount of plastic waste is found on the shorelines, on the seabed, and suspended in the water column. The Bay of Bengal and the South China Sea are the new plastic hotspots in Asia and the Bay of Bengal is more polluted than the Indian Ocean gyre. This is due to population pressure, poor waste management practices followed by the regional countries and above all poorly designed products.

The dangers of excessive plastic use and its dumping into the sea are high on the agenda of several countries. The Bay of Bengal countries individually and collectively would have to address this problem. For instance, in Bangladesh, since 2013, under Project Aware and its 'Fighting Marine debris' programme, divers and volunteers engage in survey and removal of marine debris off the Saint Martin's Island. In February 2016, the divers removed 1048 objects and of these, 90.31 per cent were of plastic. It is useful to mention that at least four of the 17 Sustainable Development Goals are closely associated with marine litter and Target 14.1 addresses prevention and reduction of marine pollution, in particular from land-based activities, including marine debris.

It is now widely acknowledged that marine littering is a 'common concern of humankind' and the key to reducing future dumping of plastic into the sea can be achieved by raising awareness amongst the international community, fishermen and coastal communities. In this context, the Bay of Bengal Initiative for Multi-Sectoral Technical and Economic Cooperation (BIMSTEC) is an appropriate regional organisation which should take the lead and give priority to plastic litter pollution. At the national level, Bay of Bengal littoral states would have to institute measures to collect plastic litter from waterfronts, promote recycling and encourage use of biodegradable packaging.

Ballast Water Management (BWM) Convention: Late Implementation, Huge Impact

Ballast water is used to stabilize the ships and is essential for the hydrodynamic safety of the ship. Ships fill in ballast water in their tanks after unloading the cargo at the destination port and then discharge it prior to reaching the source port. During this process, a large number of marine organisms such as bacteria, microbes, small invertebrates, eggs and larvae are transferred from their native location to a foreign environment. In the process, there is a persistent danger that these organisms may become invasive species and could wipe out local biodiversity, thereby permanently changing the native marine environment. The problem of invasive species has been observed across the world and is expected to grow further due to the expansion in seaborne trade and new routes taken by ships. It is estimated that upto 5 billion tonnes of ballast water is transferred annually throughout the world and approximately 10,000 unwanted species are carried in ships ballast tanks daily. Ballast water is hence widely recognised as a major environmental threat as it endangers the sensitive marine ecosystems and may lead to irreversible damage to marine life.

In order to prevent the unhindered flow of marine organisms across the oceans, standards and procedures for management of ballast water have to be implemented so as to minimize the transfer of harmful aquatic organisms. Article 196 of the UN Convention on the Law of the Sea, 1982 relates to 'use of technologies or introduction of alien or new species' and there is a provision for introducing a legally binding mechanism to coordinate a global response to this issue. Under this Article, "States shall take all measures necessary to prevent, reduce and control pollution of the marine environment resulting from the use of technologies under their jurisdiction or control, or the intentional or accidental introduction of species, alien or new, to a particular part of the marine environment, which may cause significant and harmful changes thereto." In accordance with this clause, the

IMO adopted the 'International convention for the control and management of ships' ballast water and sediments', known as the BWM Convention by consensus in 2004. However, it took more than 11 years for countries to ratify this convention. Finland was the latest signatory to this convention in September 2016, bringing the overall country count to 52. With its accession, the combined tonnage of contracting parties crossed 35 per cent threshold (tonnage of world merchant shipping) and the convention will enter into force from 08 September 2017.

Once the BWM convention is enforced, all ships of 400 GRT and above will be required to fit an approved ballast water treatment system onboard the ship. Ships would need to have a ship specific BWM plan approved by the maritime administration and this will be verified by issue of an international BWM certificate. The BWM plan includes a detailed description of the actions which need to be taken to implement the ballast water exchange standard and the ballast water performance standard for ships. Under the regulation for ballast water exchange, all ships should conduct ballast water exchange at least 200 nm from the nearest land and in water at least 200 metres in depth. Further, all ships shall remove and dispose of sediments from spaces designated to carry ballast water in accordance with the provisions of the ships' ballast water management plan. The ship will also have to maintain a ballast water record book which would record the time and location of taking or discharging the ballast water and the type of treatment which is undertaken on-board a ship.

According to the existing guidelines, BWM systems onboard ships shall discharge less than 10 viable organisms per cubic metre (greater than or equal to 50 micrometres in size) and less than 10 viable organisms per millilitre (less than 50 micrometres and greater than or equal to 10 micrometres in size). Further, to ensure that there is minimal health impact, standards have been adopted to ensure that the discharge of the indicator microbes shall not exceed the pre-defined concentrations. More than 50 BWM systems manufactured by various companies have received type final approval certification for installation on-board ships. There are three types of ballast water treatment systems: mechanical, physical and chemical. The mechanical treatment methods include filtration and separation while physical treatment methods involve sterilisation of the ballast water by use of ozone, ultra-violet light, electric currents and heat treatment. Chemical treatment methods include addition of biocides to ballast water to kill organisms.

The IMO Secretary General has termed the BWM convention as a significant step towards preservation of the marine environment but complying with the convention would pose a huge challenge for the shipping industry. The convention will impact ship-owners as they will have to retrofit the ballast water treatment systems at an additional cost. It is estimated that around 60-70,000 ships would have to be fitted with approved ballast water treatment system. It will also lead to an increase in the sales of ballast water treatment systems and the time spent to retrofit the system on operational ships will lead to loss of productivity for shipping companies. Ship operators will have to train seafarers to take various measures to comply with the new regulations when the ship is underway. Ship designers and ship builders will have to modify the existing design for optimising the fitment and for system integration of the ballast water treatment equipment and systems onboard ships. Ports where cleaning and repair of ballast tanks are undertaken will need additional facilities for reception of sediments from ballast water tanks. Maritime administrations of flag states will have to make extra arrangements for inspection of vessels including sampling of ballast water and for verification of documents. Port state control would have to train their staff for detecting the violation of regulations and for collecting evidence apart from having to issue additional documents in a routine manner.

The BWM convention does not apply to warships and hence there are no implications for the navies. India acceded to the BWM convention in 2015 and the Union Cabinet approved the introduction of the Merchant Shipping (Amendment) Bill, 2015 in May 2015. The bill provides for penalty on the violation/non-compliance to the regulations contained in the convention and there is a provision for the ports to charge the visiting ships for the use of additional facilities. Further, Indian ships below 400 GT plying within the territorial waters of India shall be issued an Indian Ballast Water Management Certificate instead of an international certificate and have to follow all regulations under the convention in Indian waters.

The BWM convention is likely to significantly lower the negative environmental impact from shipping and is an important step in environmentally safe shipping. It directly contributes to Sustainable Development Goal (SDG) 14 on sustainably using the oceans. However there are many implications for the shipping industry and maritime actors will have to cooperate to overcome the challenges for implementing the convention seamlessly across the globe.

IMO decisions to enhance the Blue Economy

The 70th session of the Marine Environment Protection Committee (MEPC) was held from 24-28 October 2016, at International Maritime Organisation (IMO) Headquarters in London. The meeting adopted key decisions which are likely to have a long lasting effect on the marine environment and would contribute to enhancing the Blue Economy.

Among these, three landmark decisions deserve a mention:

Date of implementation of global sulphur cap

Ships use Heavy Fuel Oil (HFO) which has high sulphur content and contributes to air pollution in the form of sulphur oxide (SOx) emissions. Under regulation 14 of Annex VI to MARPOL73/78 adopted in 2010 (applicable to all 171 IMO member states), the limit on the use of sulphur content in fuel used onboard ships has been progressively reduced from 4.5 per cent (mass/mass) in 2011 to 3.5 per cent on 01 Jan 2012 and this limit was to be further lowered to 0.5 per cent in 2020. However, there was a provision in the regulations that the date of implementation could be deferred from 2020 to 01 Jan 2025. This decision was to be finalized by 2018 and was subject to an assessment of the availability of sufficient quantity of low sulphur fuel.

In order to limit SOx emissions, ships have the option of choosing amongst three alternate measures: first, to use low-sulphur compliant fuels such as Marine Gas Oil (MGO) or Marine Diesel Oil (MDO); second, to switch to liquefied natural gas or biofuels such as methanol by using dual fuel engines; and third, to use exhaust gas "scrubbers", which prevent the release of SOx emissions into the atmosphere. While ships were free to choose the most feasible technical option, it was a decision which was often based on the cost of implementing the solution.

The ambiguity in the date of implementation of the 0.5 per cent limit, was leading to uncertainty in the minds of ship owners who were undecided about which technology to install onboard new ships which were yet to be ordered. On the other hand, this uncertainty was also reflected on the investment decisions of oil refiners who were unsure about the demand of low sulfur fuel for the shipping industry and were hesitating to invest in modification of the refineries which would enable them to produce bulk quantities of low sulfur fuel for the shipping industry. With the finalization of the decision for implementing the 01 Jan 2020 deadline, there is no further regulatory uncertainty and oil refineries can now invest in suitable infrastructure to meet the anticipated increase in the demand of low sulfur fuel for shipping. It also gives various actors and stakeholders time to prepare for a smooth transition to lower emissions. With this far reaching decision, it is hoped that sufficient measures can be implemented well in time so that there are no spikes in the cost of low sulphur fuel closer to 01 Jan 2020. While the supply and growth in the demand of clean fuels is a 'waiting game' between refiners and ship owners, the writing on the wall is evident that the demand for clean fuels will continue to grow during transition of the shipping industry.

The price of the low sulfur fuel is expected to higher by 50-100 per cent than the HFO (a slightly lower cost differential exists for other alternatives to lower SOx emissions) which would lead to increased cost of operations for ship charters, implying lower profits. In order to offset the high cost of low sulfur fuel it is likely that freight rates would be increased leading to an overall increase in the cost of transportation by ships. On the other hand, this is likely to encourage adoption of green shipping and would stir investments in ship efficiency.

Roadmap for reducing GHG emissions from ships

The IMO has been leading efforts to lower GHG emissions from shipping and in 2011 it was the first industrial sector to adopt mandatory energy-efficiency measures. As a consequence, by the year 2025, all new ships built will be 30 per cent more energy efficient than those built in 2014. Continuing its efforts, the MEPC approved a 'Roadmap' for developing a "Comprehensive IMO strategy on reduction of GHG emissions from ships" which would be applicable from 2017 through to 2023. The approved strategy follows a three-step approach and would be adopted in 2018. The first step involves 'data collection', which would be followed by 'data analyses' in phase 2. These would form the basis for 'policy decisions' in phase 3. Various activities are planned with relevant timelines including implementation schedules as part of the three-step approach for improving energy efficiency onboard ships.

Adoption of data collection system for fuel oil consumption

As the first step of the strategy, the MEPC adopted an amendment to chapter 4 of MARPOL Annex VI which would enter into force on 01 March 2018. Under the new Regulation 22A on collection and reporting of ship fuel oil consumption data, it is now mandatory for ships of 5,000 gross tonnage and above to collect, record and report the fuel consumption data used onboard ships, the cargo carried, and the distance travelled in each voyage. This data would have to be reported to the flag State at the end of each calendar year for verification which will then report the compiled data to the IMO ship fuel oil consumption database.

The mandatory reporting of fuel consumption data addresses a vital data gap and would enable a detailed assessment and analysis of energy efficiency onboard ships. As evident from the IMO GHG 3 study, there was some uncertainty in calculating emissions from shipping due to lack of consistent fuel consumption data. It is hoped that this amendment will provide reliable data over the next few years which would help the IMO to take an informed decision about the fair share of the shipping sector to mitigate GHG emissions under the Paris climate agreement.

The landmark decisions taken by the IMO has reduced policy uncertainty and signals a clear intent that the shipping industry is committed to environmental protection. These efforts also contribute to the UN Sustainable Development Goal (SDG) 13 on combatting climate change as well as SDG 14 on using the oceans for sustainable development. The IMO decisions are likely to encourage investments, infuse new technology, generate jobs and spur innovation thereby catalyzing the development of the Blue Economy.

International Cooperative Approaches

International Developments in Blue Economy

Given the economic potential of the oceans and the seas, a number of countries are investing enormous fiscal, technological and human capital to develop maritime economies and are marshaling in their unique strengths. Several countries have announced initiatives and action plans to promote Blue Economy. Among the island states, Seychelles and Mauritius have been spearheading the discourse while the European Union has developed a sophisticated framework for harnessing the oceans. Similarly, multilateral institutions such as Asia Pacific Economic Cooperation (APEC), East Asia Summit (EAS), South Asian Association for Regional Cooperation (SAARC) and Indian Ocean Rim Association (IORA) have highlighted Blue Economy in their statements, and communiqués.

India

The Indian government has endorsed Blue Economy and Prime Minister Narendra Modi has on a number of occasions at the national and international levels promoted the idea. He likened the "blue Chakra, the wheel in the national flag to represent the potential of the Blue Economy and endorsed Blue Economy as a new pillar of economic activity in the coastal areas and in linked hinterlands through sustainable tapping of oceanic resources and announced his vision for the seas through Security and Growth for All in the Region (SAGAR). The maiden Maritime India Summit 2016 in Mumbai witnessed investment commitments of nearly Rs 83,000 crore (US $13 billion) in the shipping, ports and allied sectors. The government plans to invest Rs 12 lakh crore over the next ten years to develop 27 industrial clusters, and to improve connectivity with ports through new rail and road projects. These are expected to create 'immense employment opportunities' in the ports, roads and shipping sectors over and above the 10 million potential jobs (four million direct and six million indirect jobs) over the next ten years under the Sagarmala project. The priority sectors for India's maritime ecosystem include shipping, Shipping, Ports, CFS/ICDs & SEZs, Road, Rail & Coastal connectivity, Shipbuilding, Investments, Advisory, Technology, Training and Leisure Including Cruise and Lighthouse Tourism.

People's Republic of China

The People's Republic of China has a Five-Year Development Plan for National Marine Economy which monitors progress of various marine sectors and the State Oceanic Administration (SOA) is the nodal agency. During 2011 and 2015, China's ocean economy grew at an annual average growth of 8.1 per cent. In 2015, the marine economy was estimated to be 6.47 trillion yuan ($989.3 billion), which is 7 per cent higher than the 2014 data. This corresponds to about 9.6 per cent of the national GDP for 2015. The marine industry employs an estimated 35.9 million people.

The Chinese leadership is conscious of the importance of the marine economy and has noted that 'A developed marine economy is an important part of building maritime power.' In March 2016, the Chinese Government announced the 13th Five-Year Plan (2016-2020) which aims to achieve nearly 100 targets to be accomplished over the five-year period and China plans to develop smart ports, construct more ice-breaking vessels, transform the ship equipment industry and engage in deep-sea activities. These initiatives will help China to promote the growth of Blue Economy.

Bangladesh

Bangladesh is perhaps the most vocal country in South Asia about Blue Economy. In 2014, it proposed 'Bay of Bengal Partnership for Blue Economy' for an "inclusive and people-centric," sustainable development of sea based resources. Blue Economy is high on national economic agenda and nearly 30 million people in Bangladesh are "dependent on the sea for livelihood, and are engaged in fishing and commercial transportation". Bangladesh is in early stages of embracing the Blue Economy and confronts a number of technological and financial constraints to make the dream come true. It has instituted several measures including setting up a research institutes for study of marine science, oceanography and training human resource to develop skills for the sustainable development of resources. It has also established scientific collaboration with other countries to develop expertise on Blue Economy.

Seychelles, Mauritius and Maldives

Seychelles and Mauritius are Small Island Developing States (SIDS) and highly dependent on the seas for economic well-being. Their economies are closely linked to the African economies who themselves have endorsed Blue Economy. Further, they have established partnership for development of Blue Economy with Australia and India and are seeking support for technical, fiscal and security related capacity building. Likewise,Maldives is highly dependent on the seas for its economic vitality and is a strong supporter of Blue Economy.

United States

The United States has the largest EEZ in the world which endows it with enormous potential for sea based economic growth. Unlike many other countries, the United States makes distinction between coastal economy and ocean economy. The coastal economy is primarily an urban economy and its thirty coastal states with population of 255.8 million (82 per cent of the U.S.) employs over 107.3 million (82 per cent of the U.S.) and contribute nearly US $13 trillion (83 per cent of the U.S.) GDP. The ocean economy (in 2010) comprised over 2.7 million jobs and contributed over US $258 billion (2.7 per cent) to the GDP of the United States. The Tourism & Recreation sector was the largest sector by both employment and GDP. The US has set up the National Ocean Economics Program (NOEP) which measures key economic indicators of the coastal and the ocean economy.

The European Union

In 2012, the European Union announced its 'Blue Growth' strategy for sustainable development of marine and maritime sectors to contribute to the Europe 2020 strategy for smart, sustainable and inclusive growth. The strategy pivots on three pillars (a) develop aquaculture, coastal tourism, marine biotechnology, and seabed mining sectors that have a high potential for sustainable jobs and growth; (b) provide marine knowledge to improve access to information about the sea, marine spatial planning for an efficient and sustainable management of activities at sea, and integrated maritime surveillance to give authorities a better picture of what is happening at sea; (c) foster cooperation between countries. For the European Union, the Blue Economy represents roughly 5.4 million jobs and generates a gross added value of almost €500 billion a year.

Multilateral Institutions

Blue Economy has gathered momentum at the multilateral level. The 2014 Perth Communiqué of the Indian Ocean Rim Association (IORA) of October 2014 notes the Indian Ocean countries are 'strengthening the Blue Economy' through sustainable development of fisheries, judicious exploitation of minerals, harnessing renewable energy and encouraging coastal tourism to 'stimulate growth and improve food and energy security' as a 'common source of growth, innovation and job creation'. A text of the 'Perth Principles' is placed at Appendix. The concept is also percolating into other groupings such as the South Asian Association for Regional Cooperation (SAARC), BIMSTEC and ASEAN. Cooperation among maritime nations is a vital ingredient for development of the Blue Economy and multilateral institutions are a strong medium to enhance the development of the Blue Economy.

Cooperative Approaches to promote the Blue Economy: Regional Maritime Emission Control Areas (ECAs)

Introduction

The 'Blue Economy' endorses sustainable development of the seas and oceans and attempts to balance social, environmental and economic goals while promoting exploration and utilization of oceanic resources. The concept has found widespread acceptance amongst coastal countries and island states and Prime Minister Modi has called for regional cooperation to support India's vision of the Blue Economy.

Shipping is a central pillar of the Blue Economy and growth in shipping is a prerequisite for enhanced maritime trade. The Blue Economy promotes shipping which is the cheapest and the most energy efficient mode for transportation of goods especially over long distances. Shipping also has the least CO_2 emission intensity (emissions per distance travelled) as compared to other modes of transport such as rail, road and air and a modal shift to coastal shipping has been suggested for reducing emissions from the transport sector. The shipping sector employs a large number of seafarers directly and the livelihood of many people is indirectly dependent on shipping which contributes to the social dimension of the Blue Economy.

Impact of Shipping on Air Pollution

Most ships use Heavy Fuel Oil (HFO) which is a residual fuel left after the distillation of crude oil. Use of HFO onboard ships results in emission of air pollutants like oxides of sulphur (SOx) and oxides of nitrates (NOx), Particulate Matter (PM) and other greenhouse gases (GHG) such as methane, carbon monoxide (CO), carbon dioxide (CO_2) and non-methane volatile organic compounds (NMVOC). Emissions from combustion of HFO especially near the coastline and in ports contributes to local air pollution in coastal areas leading to reduced visibility, acid rain, damage to plants and have severe effects such as respiratory problems and eye irritation in humans contributing to premature deaths. Apart from emitting 796 million tons of CO_2 (yearly average in period 2007-2012) which contributed to 3.1 per cent of global CO_2 emissions, the shipping sector also emitted 10 million tons of SOx and 18 million tons of NOx emissions (equivalent to 13 per cent and 15 per cent of global SOx and NOx emissions respectively). The weak environmental performance of the shipping industry is detrimental to the goal of the Blue Economy and needs to be addressed.

ECAs and limits of sulfur in fuel used onboard ships

While growth of the shipping industry is essential for continued growth of the world economy, it is equally important to control air emissions from the sector. With this aim, the International Maritime Organisation (IMO) adopted certain agreements under the International Convention for the Prevention of Pollution from ships (MARPOL) Annex VI. Under this Annex various regulations to lower CO_2 emissions by improving energy efficiency onboard ships and to lower NOx and SOx emissions were adopted.

In order to minimize airborne emissions, specific areas in the Baltic Sea and North Sea were designated as Emission Control Areas (ECAs) in 2005 where stringent control on use of sulfur in fuel was exercised. In 2010, these areas were expanded to the North American ECA, which included most of US and Canadian coast and to the US Caribbean. IMO regulations were also framed to lower the use of sulfur in fuel used onboard ships globally and different limits inside and outside the ECAs which are have been enforced are shown in Table 1.

Table 1: Permissible limits of sulfur in fuel used onboard ships

Outside ECA	Inside ECA
50 per cent m/m prior to 1 January 2012	50 per cent m/m prior to 1 July 2010
50 per cent m/m on and after 1 January 2012	1.00 per cent m/m on and after 1 July 2010
50 per cent m/m on and after 1 January 2020*	0.10 per cent m/m on and after 1 January 2015
*This date will be finalised in 2018 and could be deferred to 1 January 2025 Note: per cent m/m has to be multiplied by 10,000 to convert to ppm	

Prior to 01 Jan 2012, there were no regulations and ships used HFO with a sulfur content which could be higher than 4.5 per cent m/m (by weight). This is equivalent to 45,000 ppm (parts per million) as against a permitted level of 10 ppm in diesel (Euro V standard) for cars!! This was lowered to 3.5 per cent m/m after 01 Jan 2012 and is scheduled to be limited to 0.50 per cent m/m after 1 January 2020. More stringent limits are applicable inside the ECAs (shown in column 2 of Table 1), which has resulted in the lowering of local pollution in port cities located inside the ECAs in Europe and the US.

Declaration of ECAs in Chinese ports

ECA help in improving the air quality in port cities and coastal areas. While four areas limiting the use of sulfur have been designated by the IMO, other countries such as Japan, Australia and EU are considering adoption of ECAs. More recently, China has announced its plan to lower the content of sulfur in fuel being used onboard ships entering Chinese waters. Three maritime ECAs have been declared by China: The Yangtze River Delta, the Zhujiang (Pearl River) Delta, and an area in the Bohai Sea. 11 key ports of Shanghai, Ningbo-Zhoushan, Suzhou, Nantong, Shenzhen, Guangzhou, Zhuhai, Tianjin, Qinhuangdao, Tangshan and Huaye are included in the ECA along with inland navigable waters under the jurisdiction of 38 major Chinese cities. The proposed regulations which were promulgated in December 2015 would be applicable to all merchant ships navigating, anchored or underway in the promulgated area but naval ships, sport ships and fishing vessels are exempted.

In the first phase of the plan, which is applicable from 01 January to 31 Dec 2016, ships entering the ECAs may be required to limit the content of sulfur in the fuel to 0.5 per cent m/m or below. Under this provision the Shanghai, Jiangsu and Zhejiang maritime safety administration (MSA) falling under the Yangtze River Delta ECA have promulgated that commencing 01 April 2016, ships berthing alongside jetties in Shanghai, Ningbo-Zhoushan, Suzhou and Nantong ports have to use low sulfur fuels or face fines and penalties. This initiative is planned to be extended in a phased manner to other ports and mandatory requirements are likely to be enforced for all ports in designated areas from 01 Jan 2017.

A Strong Case for Promoting Regional Maritime ECAs

China's declaration of maritime ECAs is a bold initiative for cleaning the air in port cities. Such measures to include the cost of environmental externalities into the cost of shipping operations have sent a clear forward looking signal to the shipping industry. With this move, China, has also demonstrated that clean environment and economic growth can be pursued simultaneously. It has also set an example to other developing countries such as India, Malaysia and Indonesia to think about solutions which balances environmental protection, economic growth and social progress in accordance with the objectives of the Blue Economy.

It is important to note that Singapore and Hong Kong ports which compete for markets in the same region have also adopted a limit of 0.5 per cent m/m of sulfur in fuel used onboard ships through issue of local port regulations. Strict enforcement of these regulations is anticipated which will result in cleaner ships visiting these ports. As the shipping market is cost conscious, it is anticipated that ships having poor environmental performance would be attracted to ports which are not covered under these regulations in Bangladesh, India, Myanmar, Sri Lanka, Indonesia and other countries in the region.

In order to curtail this development there is a strong case for regional cooperation for voluntary adoption of maritime ECAs in South Asia, South East Asia and other littoral countries in the Indian Ocean Region. The IORA, BIMSTEC, ASEAN and other multilateral regional institutions provides a suitable platform for discussion on these issues and for sharing the best practices and country experiences from these initiatives.

Consequences and Impacts

Promulgation of the ECA regulations reflects the intent of the governments to clean the local air in large port cities. The Chinese initiative is well structured and advances the date of enforcement of the 0.5 per cent m/m limit for sulphur content in fuels which would be applicable from 2020 globally. The cumulative environmental benefits accrued out of these measures for port cities have also been enhanced due to advancing the dates of implementation.

In order to comply with the regulations, ships may use equivalent measures to reduce SOx emissions such as use of scrubbers and use of alternate fuels such as marine gas oil (MGO), marine diesel oil (MDO) and liquefied natural gas (LNG). This may lead to growth of ancillary industry to provide these services in port cities and would attract inflow of new technology and investment along with additional jobs.

The regulations are likely to encourage ships to use electricity from the port (cold ironing). This would give a boost to electricity demand from ships berthed alongside jetties. This power can be supplied from large scale super-efficient power plants located outside cities or from renewable energy, thereby giving a boost to these industries and local economy apart from meeting the primary objective of lowering airborne emission from ships inside harbour.

While adopting low sulphur, fuels would lead to significant reduction in emissions of SOx in port cities, it will come at a cost. Alternate fuels such as MDO and MGO are approximately 40 per cent more costly than HFO (spot price at Singapore) which will directly lead to increase in the cost of ship charter. However, this is a small price to pay for cleaning the air and it is anticipated that the health benefits will be much higher than the cost of implementation of these measures.

Challenges

The success of the ECA depends critically on three aspects: legal backing for the regulations, enforcement and monitoring capability and availability of specific fuel and appropriate technology for retro fitment onboard ships. In this regard, there are a few challenges which need to be overcome. As the governments, have promulgated these regulations in their areas of jurisdiction, both foreign vessels and vessels registered in the country have to follow the promulgated rules when in the declared zones. However, the implementation and enforcement of the regulation would entail a large administrative cost for monitoring ships. Further, while ships are mandated to maintain bunker delivery notes and preserving oil samples for one year under these regulations, checking these would involve a significant amount of time and effort from the maritime agencies.

The availability of requisite amount of fuel with low sulfur content is also an area of concern and refineries have to make significant investments to produce a higher quantity of low sulfur HFO. This is also a cause of concern for global refineries and the uncertainty over the growth in demand of low sulfur HFO may reduce once a decision is taken (in 2018) on the final date of implementation of the 0.50 per cent m/m limit in non ECA areas. If the date of implementing of the global regulation is retained as 1 January 2020, it would lead to substantial investments and modifications by refineries to enhance the production of low sulfur HFO to meet the anticipated demand of the shipping industry, albeit at a higher cost. But availability of low sulfur HFO in the short term continues to remain a challenge.

Conclusion

Voluntary adoption of clean fuels used onboard ships is now showing an increasing trend. While global adoption of such regulations is difficult due to the different capabilities of countries, a regional approach may be an intermediate step towards a global adoption. It is therefore appropriate that a cooperative approach to lower sulfur content in fuels is supported by India under the Blue Economy agenda. The success of the scheme however, would critically depend on the strict enforcement of the ECA among all countries and the availability of requisite quality of fuel at low prices.

Blue Economy: Expanding India-US Maritime Cooperation

The contemporary Maritime discourse on India US relations is highly skewed towards strategic issues led by the recent signing of the Logistics Exchange Memorandum of Agreement (LEMOA), and two other similar agreements are under active consideration by the two sides. Also, several other bilateral maritime agreements relating to technical arrangement for sharing of information on merchant shipping, maritime security dialogue, agreement on India as a major defence partner, and defence technology and trade initiative (DTTI) have been signed. In essence, strategic, Defense and Security ties form the 'bedrock of the bilateral strategic partnership' a fact both sides acknowledge.

While these have no doubt contributed to the robustness of India-US strategic partnership, several other maritime and marine issues are also resonating in the joint statements and bilateral discussions, and merit attention. In this context, the Joint Statement on the Second India-U.S. Strategic and Commercial Dialogue held in New Delhi in August 2016 makes specific reference to India-US marine cooperation on two specific issues; first, the 'Our Ocean Conference' in Washington D.C. on 15-16 September 2016, whose focus is on key ocean issues such as marine protected areas, sustainable fisheries, marine pollution, and climate-related impacts on the ocean; and second, the first India U.S. Oceans Dialogue later this year.

These initiatives can potentially strengthen cooperation in marine science, ocean energy, managing and protecting ocean biodiversity, marine pollution, and sustainable use of ocean resources, which are the constituents of Blue Economy. Both countries have made serious note of the prospects for the development of Blue Economy at the national level and these finds reference in the respective agenda and action plans for the sustainable development of resources, mitigation of climate change and Environment and Ecological discourses, and job creation.

The US does not use the term Blue Economy; instead it makes distinction between coastal economy and ocean economy. The coastal economy is primarily an urban economy and the thirty coastal states with population of 255.8 million (82 per cent of the U.S.) employ over 107.3 million (82 per cent of the U.S.) and contribute nearly US $13 trillion (83 per cent of the U.S. GDP). The ocean economy (2010) comprised over 2.7 million jobs and contributed over $258 billion (2.7 per cent) to the GDP of the United States. The tourism and recreation sector was the largest sector by both employment and GDP. The US has set up the National Ocean Economics Program (NOEP), which measures key Economic indicators of the coastal and the ocean economy and the Ocean Economy Accounting System (OEAS).

India has also announced national initiatives and action plans to promote Blue Economy. The maiden Maritime India Summit 2016 in Mumbai witnessed investment commitments of nearly Rs 83,000 crore (US $13 billion) in the shipping, ports and allied sectors. The Government plans to invest Rs 12 lakh crore over the next ten years to develop 27 industrial clusters, and to improve connectivity with ports through new rail and road projects. These are expected to create 'immense employment opportunities' in the ports, roads and shipping sectors over and above the 10 million potential jobs (four million direct and six million indirect jobs) over the next ten years under the Sagarmala project. The priority sectors for India's Blue Economy ecosystem include shipping, ports, CFS/ICDs & SEZs, Road, Rail & Coastal connectivity, Shipbuilding, Investments, Advisory, Technology, Training and Leisure Including Cruise and Lighthouse Tourism.

There are at last four issues which can contribute to the India-US Maritime Cooperation. First, is sharing the expertise and knowledge for the development of Blue Economy. The Center for the Blue Economy at the Monterey Institute of International Studies undertakes three major activities i.e. research, education, and outreach. It is mandated to promote ocean and coastal sustainability by providing the best available information to empower governments, NGOs, businesses, and concerned citizens to make educated decisions about the marine environment.

Second, the accounting system for measuring the Blue Economy; India does not have an accounting systems which will help locate Blue Economy within the broader national economy. The NOEP and the OEAS would significantly help India develop a system for computation and evaluation of the Blue Economy

Third, share expertise on select Blue Economy sectors such as marine leisure and recreational industry, which is also one of the thrust areas in the national plan to develop Blue Economy. The tourism & recreation sector has nine industries and is by far the largest sector in the US and accounts for 94 per cent of 2010 sector employment and 92 per cent of the GDP. Similarly, the offshore-renewable energy (wind, tide, wave, solar) industries including desalination are priority areas for the Indian government. For instance, 'The Pipe' project is a good example of a sustainable infrastructure capable of generating 10,000 MWh annually which in turn produce 4.5 billion litres of drinking water for California.

Fourth, unlike the established industries that support the Blue Economy for which datasets can be generated, there are a number of non-market services which contribute to national economy, need evaluation. These include the ocean and coastal assets such as coastal wetlands and estuaries that are referred to as carbon sinks contribute in tens of billions of dollars annually. The non-market value of these can rival the established ocean and coastal extractive and service industries and these will grow in the future as we obtain better understanding of the marine ecosystem services.

Fourth, unlike the established industries that support the Blue Economy for which datasets can be generated, there are a number of non-market services which contribute to national economy, need evaluation. These include the ocean and coastal assets such as coastal wetlands and estuaries that are referred to as carbon sinks contribute in tens of billions of dollars annually. The non-market value of these can rival the established ocean and coastal extractive and service industries and these will grow in the future as we obtain better understanding of the marine ecosystem services.

South China Sea Arbitration Award and SDG 2030

The South China Sea Arbitration Award of 12 July 2016 has implicated China for large-scale reclamation and construction of artificial islands in the Spratly Islands. The award observed that China had 'violated its obligation" to preserve and protect the marine environment in the South China Sea and caused 'irreparable harm to the coral reef habitat'. In this context, two multilateral initiatives i.e. Xiamen Declaration and Sustainable Development Goals 2030, merit attention.

The Xiamen Declaration

The 2014 Leaders' Declaration at the 22nd APEC Economic Leaders' Meeting endorsed the Xiamen Declaration which identifies four priority areas for collaborated and concerted actions on:

(a) Coastal and marine ecosystem conservation and disaster resilience;

(b) Role of the ocean on food security and food-related trade;

(c) Marine science, technology and innovation;

(d) Blue Economy.

There are at least five important reasons to recall the Xiamen Declaration and implement it in the South China Sea. First is about food security. The South China Sea has abundant quantities of fish (3,365 species comprising 263 families) and is an important source of protein for people in China and Southeast Asia. The region has been assessed as one of the top five most productive fishing zones in the world with a yearly catch (reported and unreported) of nearly 16.6 million tons annually. In the coming decades, as populations increase in China and Southeast Asia, there will be higher demand for food and the sea-based food chain would be the best source for protein supplement.

The second issue relates to exploitation of non-living resources such as oil and gas, salt, minerals etc. According to one estimate, the South China Sea may contain nearly 3-3.5 billion barrels of oil and 65-70 trillion cubic feet (1.4-2 trillion cubic meters) of natural gas. However, there are a number of environmental risks to offshore energy exploration and production arising from oil spills and accidents involving ships carrying oil and gas. These can be mitigated by developing an oil spill response strategy for South China Sea by the littoral states.

The third issue is about the wellbeing of the coastal communities that are dependent on the South China Sea marine life for their livelihoods. Nearly 55 per cent of the world's fishing vessels operate in the South China Sea and the fishing industry in the region employs nearly 3.7 million people who are dependent on it for their livelihoods. Perhaps the single most important issue for these communities is fisheries management mechanisms and robust checks on over exploitation of fish which in the past has led to depleted stock directly affecting livelihoods.

The fourth issue concerns the necessity to preserve biodiversity and protecting the marine ecosystem in the South China Sea to help support a vibrant marine life, protect against degradation of ecosystems, stem biodiversity loss, and ensure improved food security. A regular process of reporting and assessment of the state of the marine environment including education on ecology would raise awareness among the fishermen. This can be achieved through a variety of bilateral and multilateral mechanisms such as regional fisheries programme under the UN Food and Agriculture Organization would contribute to the health of the oceans. It is useful to mention that coral reefs provide goods and services worth $375 billion annually and marine biodiversity is considered as a future medicine chest. Many drugs are now being developed from coral reefs as possible cures for cancer, arthritis, human bacterial infections, viruses, and other diseases.

Fifth, the South China Sea Arbitration Award has stated that there is no legal basis for China to claim historic rights to resources within the nine-dash line, and Beijing's argument that the features of the South China Sea are entitled to exclusive economic zones was dismissed. This will result in large sea spaces around the Spratly Islands that would fall under Marine areas beyond national jurisdiction, commonly referred to as the high seas where no one nation has sole responsibility for management. China can initiate bilateral and multilateral approaches to help foster ecosystem resilience and promote mitigation and adaptation strategies for robust management of marine ecosystems.

United Nations Sustainable Development Goals 2030

In 2015, the United Nations announced the Sustainable Development Goals (SDGs) to 'end poverty, protect the planet, and ensure prosperity for all and address Climate Change' through integrated and indivisible 17 Goals with 169 associated targets. Goal 14, titled "Conserve and sustainably use the oceans, seas and marine resources for sustainable development" lists 14 targets to be achieved over the next 15 years up to 2030 to help ensure good health of the oceans as also contribute to the sustainable use of marine resources for economic growth and human well-being.

These targets can be placed into two closely associated baskets i.e. health of the oceans and the fisheries. There are a number of risks to the health of the oceans due to marine pollution, ocean acidification and damage to coastal and marine areas. As regards fisheries, SDGs call for regulated harvesting and to curb overfishing and illegal unreported and unregulated (IUU) fishing. Further, efforts must be made to provide access to small-scale artisanal fishers to marine resources and markets.

What Next

After initial refutation and rancorous pronouncements on the validity of the award, China is wooing the Philippines economically and according to Philippines Defence Minister Chinese Coast Guard ships have not been sighted in waters around the Scarborough Shoal thereby allowing unimpeded access to the Philippine's fishermen. These are significant developments and may have resulted in a relatively quieter environment in the South China Sea.

However, the litmus test for China is whether it is willing to work with regional countries to restore the damaged marine environment. It is beyond doubt that the Chinese activities in the South China Sea have left behind an unacceptable adverse ecological footprint and are indefensible.

Maritime Governance and Capacity Building

Strengthening Ocean Governance: Marine Genetic Resources (MGR) in Areas Beyond National Jurisdiction (ABNJ)

The 1982 UN Convention on the Law of the Seas provides the legal framework for governance of the oceans and the seas within which, all activities must be carried out. Areas Beyond National Jurisdiction (ABNJ), are those areas of the oceans for which no one nation has sole responsibility for management. These include the 'High Seas' (areas beyond the Exclusive Economic Zone (EEZ) of a country) and 'The Area' (seabed beyond the continental shelf). In the context of resources, ABNJ includes the water column beyond the EEZ of a country and all living resources contained therein and seabed resources beyond the continental shelf of the coastal state. Approximately, 64 per cent of the surface of the oceans and 95 per cent of its volume fall under the ABNJ and conservation and protection of these areas is extremely difficult and challenging.

Advances in technology coupled with increasing demand for resources has led to a gradual increase in the exploitation of the oceans for mineral and biological resources. While 'Marine Protected Areas' and regional fisheries agreements do exist, less than half a per cent of marine habitats are protected as compared to 11.5 per cent of global land area making ABNJ as one of the least protected areas on this planet. Over years, it was also recognized that the existing framework of regulations do not sufficiently address the conservation and sustainable use of marine biodiversity in the ABNJ. This is both due to 'legal gaps' as well as 'implementation gaps'.

Realizing the importance of marine biodiversity and inadequacies in governance of the ABNJ, an Ad Hoc Open Ended Informal Working Group was established by the UN General Assembly in 2004 to identify the gaps in the international legal regime. The last meeting of the working group was held in New York from 20-23 January 2015 and it recommended an international legally binding instrument under the Convention on the conservation and sustainable use of marine Biodiversity Beyond Areas of National Jurisdiction (BBNJ). As per the recommendations of the Working Group, a Preparatory Committee (PrepCom), has been established which would make substantive recommendations to the UN General Assembly on the elements of a draft text of an international legally binding instrument before the end of the seventy-second session in 2017. Based on these inputs, an intergovernmental conference may be convened under the auspices of the United Nations, to consider the recommendations on the elements and to elaborate the text of an international legally binding instrument under the Convention.

Marine Genetic Resources (MGR) which consist of the genetic material of deep sea marine sponges, krill, corals, seaweeds and bacteria are attracting increasing scientific and commercial attention due to its potential usage in medicines and cosmetics. The existing Law of the Sea regime is silent on the MGR and only refers to the 'mineral resources' in 'The Area'. The ISA regulates all activities for exploration and exploitation of the 'mineral resources' in the Area which are the common heritage of mankind (Article 136). The definition of "resources" is limited to "all solid, liquid or gaseous mineral resources in situ, in the Area, at or beneath the seabed, including poly metallic nodules". On the other hand, part VII Section 2 of the 1982 UN Convention on the Law of the Seas deals with fisheries and marine mammals in the ABNJ but does not refer to other living resources, such as those living on the seabed, or benthic ecosystems living on or near seamounts, hydrothermal vents and cold-water coral reefs. The 1982 UN Convention on the Law of the Seas therefore does not specifically regulate living resources such as MGR, in the ABNJ.

Records show that only 10 countries accounted for 90 per cent of the patents on MGR due to lack of physical access to ABNJ, technology to extract MGRs, and financial 3 resources for its commercial development. Developing countries therefore argued that free access to MGR, such as that applicable to the living resources in the high seas goes against the principle of 'just and equitable international economic order'. Hence countries from the developing world called for BBNJ to be declared as the common heritage of mankind and demanded that all countries should benefit from the economic returns by a process of benefit sharing.

These arguments are countered by developed nations which maintain that exploration and exploitation of MGR by undertaking activities such as bioprospecting falls under the right to conduct Marine Scientific Research (MSR), and is a part of the freedom of the high seas. Hence, under 1982 UN Convention on the Law of the Seas, MGR in the ABNJ is accessible to any state. Japan, US and Canada put forth the argument that research on MGR is costly and is undertaken by private companies. Hence, they have the first and the sole right to earn from the profits which they make out of commercializing MGR. Countries are also divided on the 'specific need' for explicitly defining the use of marine BBNJ and framing laws for its conservation and sustainable use as under Article 240 (d), 1982 UN Convention on the Law of the Seas already specifies that MSR has to be conducted in compliance with all relevant regulations including the general obligations for the protection and preservation of the marine environment.

It is evident that the countries need to forego some of their interests to arrive at a compromise solution in the larger interest of protection and sustainable use of the oceans. Exploitation of MGR can be governed in an arrangement similar to the control and administration of deep seabed resources by the ISA in which, half of the allocated area is handed back to the ISA after 15 years of the grant of rights to undertake exploration. The arrangement could explore mandatory joint development and scientific exploration so as to build the capacity of other developing countries. Sharing of revenues, access to relevant technology, data and research results from the development of MGR could also be explored between countries. An appropriate lay off time for exclusive commercial use of the research results from MGR could be decided and the IPR could then be surrendered for the welfare of humanity, is another model which could be explored.

The first meeting of the PrepCom was held from 28 March - 09 April 2016 at New York and was closely watched. Some of the above approaches were explored and debated. Notwithstanding the deliberations at the PrepCom, one thing is however certain that the agenda has moved on from 'exploitation' to 'sustainable use' of resources and ocean governance will play a key role in this transition.

Developing 'Software' for Blue Economy

India has announced that its march towards developing the Blue Economy has begun and "India is on the brink of a blue revolution". The Union Minister for Shipping, Road Transport and Highways has stated that the government plans to invest Rs 12 lakh crore over the next ten years to develop 27 industrial clusters, and to improve connectivity with ports through new rail and road projects. These are expected to create 'immense employment opportunities' in the ports, roads and shipping sectors over and above the 10 million potential jobs under the Sagarmala project. Though ambitious, these projects could be completed in 'half the time'. A careful review of the above statement suggests that investments are targeted for developing infrastructure, which is the 'hardware' of the Blue Economy; however, India is yet to invest in the 'software' which includes at least four segments i.e. blue laboratory; blue business; blue education; and blue skills.

Blue Economy is a combination of traditional sectors such as shipbuilding, shipping, ports and fisheries. Marine tourism or the marine leisure industry and cruise liner industry is another important sector of Blue Economy. Blue Economy also includes an assortment of new technology-oriented sectors that are capable of supporting advanced marine bio-prospecting through exploration and study of the marine ecosystems, marine organisms and animals, plants, algae and vegetation and multispecies aquaculture. These are important ingredients for a number of products which are essential as proteins in the form of food and feed, pharmaceuticals, cosmetics and other products. Besides, technologies capable of generating energy through tidal wave and sea based wind farms are already in operation.

By all counts, Blue Economy is science intensive and requires enormous fiscal resources. These have to be financed by the government or provided for by private 2 entities who are important stakeholders in the development of Blue Economy. Further, the existing models of public and private partnerships, incentive based financing, venture capital and seed money are other ways to generate capital. A blue bank which has a corpus of funds to support innovation and entrepreneurship is a useful idea. An innovative approach could also be in the form of crowd funding and fund raising campaigns to raise capital for implementing the concept.

Another important facet of the development of Blue Economy is human resource. The human capital would have to be nurtured at the grass root levels beginning with schools and colleges and thereafter during professional courses. Further, vocational institutions are critical for promoting, training and skilling workers that are adept at understanding the oceans and working in industries that support Blue Economy.

This requires a strategy for human resource development as the curriculum would have to be customized for a specific vocation. It would also be important to raise awareness among the youth and also the industry who would be the final recipients of this highly specialized gene pool of blue professionals. Further, there would be a need for sector-specific talent development for a number of white (administrative and institutional) and blue (products and services) collar jobs. This can potentially plug the gap between the demand and supply of new generation of marine scientists, professionals, technicians, and entrepreneurs. The industry can develop blue technology incubator to spur business and jobs and also invest in marine spatial planning programmes which support sustainable use of resources to ensure good health of the oceans. Likewise, the role of entrepreneurs, start-ups, medium and small enterprises cannot be underestimated. In this context, this national agenda of 'skill development', 'make in India' and 'digital India' would amply support the development of Blue Economy.

Another important facet for the growth of Blue Economy is diplomacy which can facilitate foreign investments, transfer of technology for innovation and development of blue industries through collaboration. Given that oceans have a transnational character, an integrated development of Blue Economy across regions and sub-regions can be promoted through multilateral institutions and organisations such as the South Asian Association for Regional Cooperation (SAARC), Indian Ocean Rim Association (IORA) 3 and the Bay of Bengal Initiative for Multi-Sectoral Technical and Economic Cooperation (BIMSTEC) who have also endorsed development of Blue Economy.

Although job creation is at the heart of the Blue Economy, it is the sustainable use of sea based resources that merit consideration. The focus of any blue growth strategy should directly contribute to the UN Sustainable Development Goal No. 14: "Conserve and sustainably use the oceans, seas and marine resources" which places enormous demands on states to plan, manage and use the seas sustainably by the current and future generations.

While the overarching objective is to develop Blue Economy, it should be supported by a robust regulatory framework which contributes to sustainable use of existing natural resources. Also, proactive and facilitative governance which supports job creation, encourages innovation and provides opportunities for knowledge-based businesses in key maritime sectors is indispensable. In essence, a clear national vision and a road map for 'blue revolution growth' would require a variety of stakeholders, businesses, industries, institutions, academia and the government to pool in resources to develop the 'software' of Blue Economy

Building India's Maritime Resurgence Through Citizen Engagement

A strong push has been given to the maritime agenda in India since the swearing in of Prime Minister Modi. This is evident from the range of initiatives taken by the Indian government such as Maritime India Summit-2016, announcement of 'Sagarmala' project, the push for the 'Blue Economy' agenda, outreach efforts such as Project 'Mausam' and the conduct of International Fleet Review 2016, to name a few. While the intent of the government is evident, a maritime resurgence in India requires the acceptance of the philosophy of being a maritime nation and an involvement by the citizens of India.

Maritime awareness amongst the people of the country plays a key role in building a maritime nation and the maritime thought needs to permeate to the citizens. Building such a maritime culture requires a much larger impetus and effort from the institutions of the country and it is this area in which India needs to improve. Historically India had a maritime outlook and even today 90 per cent of India's international trade in terms of volume and 77 per cent in terms of value is moved by sea. However, it appears that as a nation, the maritime thought is somewhat restricted to the coastal areas and the people of the heartland have a predominantly continental mindset. The oceans are still seen as being far away, both literally and figuratively from the center of governance and the seat of power which is concentrated in New Delhi. It is therefore no surprise that the maritime flavour appears in spurts in the policies and initiatives of the Indian government.

World Ocean Day (WOD) celebrated every year on June 08 provides us with an occasion to raise global awareness of the intrinsic value of the oceans and to educate the public on the role and importance of the oceans for life on earth. It is an opportunity to get involved in protecting the oceans by raising consciousness of how human lives depend on the oceans. The theme for WOD, 2015-16 is 'Healthy Oceans, Healthy Planet', which highlights the need to maintain healthy oceans as they are essential for food security, biodiversity, as regulators of climate and are a critical part of the biosphere. Activities such as beach cleanups, educational programs, photography contests, film and seafood festivals are organized the world over to engage the public through personal and community action. This year's theme finds resonance with the freshly minted Sustainable Development Goal 14 by the United Nations on the oceans viz. "Conserve and sustainably use the oceans, seas and marine resources for sustainable development".

However, there appears to be a lack of enthusiasm among the civil society and specialised agencies in organising events to engage the citizens of the country. In effect, there has been no major event to celebrate the WOD and an opportunity for spreading awareness on the importance of oceans for life on earth may have been missed. In contrast this day was celebrated in countries such as Australia, US, Europe, Southeast Asia and Latin America in support with various aquariums, civil society, the UNESCO and various national governments. The role of social media was also valuable and the event found a significant mention on Twitter, Instagram and online media. Various celebrities including the White House joined in spreading the message of ocean conservation via the visual media such as CNN and the National Geographic. Such dynamism was sadly missing in the Indian context

The month of June is also important for the maritime community as June 25 is celebrated as the 'Day of the Seafarer'. The campaign theme adopted by the International Maritime Organization (IMO) this year is, "At Sea for All" to highlight the important role of the seafarers in the world economy. In the words of IMO Secretary General Kitack Lim: "this year, we are once again asking people everywhere to show their appreciation for the seafarers that quietly, mostly unnoticed, keep the wheels of the world in motion". The theme for the 'Day of the Seafarer' this year is aligned with the 2016 World Maritime Day theme, "Shipping: Indispensable to the World" and emphasizes that seafarers serve at sea for providing goods and commodities to all of us – and, consequently, they are also indispensable to the world.

The worldwide population of seafarers in 2015 was estimated to be around 774,000 officers and 873,000 ratings. The total number of seafarers has increased by 34 per cent between 2005 and 2010 and further by 24 per cent from 2010 to 2015, due to the growth of the international shipping fleet and the demand for seafarers is anticipated to further grow over the next 10 years. China, Philippines, Indonesia, Russian Federation, Ukraine and India are the largest suppliers of seafarers who serve on the world merchant fleet of 68,723 ships. India has a registered strength of 62,673 seafarers and contributes significantly to the officer cadre after China and the Philippines. Despite an improvement in recruitment and reductions in officer wastage rates over the past five years, BIMCO manpower report on the global supply and demand of seafarers - 2015 predicts that the deficit in the officer cadre is likely to increase from the current 2.1 per cent to 18.3 per cent by 2025.

This outlook hints that in order to overcome the shortage that there should be a focus on the supply of qualified and competent seafarers in the future which cannot happen without concerted efforts and measures to address key manpower issues. India which has the benefit of favourable demography would do well by generating awareness on maritime issues for the millions of trained English speaking young men and women entering the workforce every year. This also needs to be followed up with sound training with hands on experience for these trainees so as to enhance their employment opportunities on merchant ships. Human capital is also a critical component of the 'Skill 4 India' mission which will benefit the 'Make in India' drive for production of ships and defence equipment in the country

This outlook hints that in order to overcome the shortage that there should be a focus on the supply of qualified and competent seafarers in the future which cannot happen without concerted efforts and measures to address key manpower issues. India which has the benefit of favourable demography would do well by generating awareness on maritime issues for the millions of trained English speaking young men and women entering the workforce every year. This also needs to be followed up with sound training with hands on experience for these trainees so as to enhance their employment opportunities on merchant ships. Human capital is also a critical component of the 'Skill 4 India' mission which will benefit the 'Make in India' drive for production of ships and defence equipment in the country

Universities, specialized institutions and nodal agencies which cut across themes such as engineering, economics, fisheries, environment, trade and ocean governance will enhance the maritime resurgence in India. Collaboration between leading thinktanks, NGOs and planning departments in the ministries with these institutes will also enhance the employability of the workforce. This future generation of seafarers will later become maritime ambassadors and will become catalysts to promote maritime thought and awareness in the country. Apart from this engaging citizen in maritime events is an activity in which the Indian government needs to invest significantly so as to revitalize the maritime resurgence in the country.

Blue Economy: Awareness, Education and Financing

The concept of Blue Economy is gaining popularity among a number of stakeholders including government agencies, scientists, academia, industry, and entrepreneurs. However, there is a need to adopt a holistic approach to develop Blue Economy, and in this context, at least ten issues merit attention.

First, there is lack of general information about the sea among the populace. The common belief and imagination of the sea is that it is an endless space and serves as a medium to transport goods and a rich source of fish. The coastal area is a place for leisure and the underwater domain is unfathomable.

Second, there are numerous knowledge gaps particularly in terms of data about sea based resources, health of the oceans, issues of biodiversity, marine and aquatic life and the impact of pollution and land based industrial discharge to marine habitats and ecosystems. This has been a result of a near absence of marine sciences in the curriculum at primary, secondary and tertiary level which limits interest among students who would in the future emerge as scientists, engineers and skilled workers. This gap can be addressed through collaboration among education and training institutions, industry and the government.

Third, is lack of marine science data for public use. Much of the data is held with scientific bodies, laboratories and research centers. These agencies are supported by the government through various programmes, funding and research infrastructure, thus there are issues of intellectual property rights and some data is considered too sensitive to be shared with the general public.

Fourth, given the above considerations, the entrepreneurs and start-ups do not possess adequate knowledge of the richness of the oceans and are unable to comprehend newer and sustainable use of the seas which inhibits innovation for Blue Economy. If marine data is made accessible and limitations on its usage are removed, the small and medium-sized enterprises (SMEs) and other private agencies are in a good position to explore possibilities to use the specific data to develop programmes such as marine spatial planning, mapping the seabed and overlying water column under national jurisdiction.

Fifth, growth of Blue Economy is highly dependent on technically skilled workforce which should be able to understand the marine medium, its unique characteristic, apply the innovative technologies in science and engineering, and fill the skills gap. Given that Blue Economy thrives on innovation, the younger the innovator, the greater will be the zeal to do something different and this enthusiasm can help achieve successful business despite numerous challenges which the innovator may encounter at the personal level as also at the ecosystem level. In essence, an innovator with an interesting idea can transform into an entrepreneur.

Sixth, is the need to develop tailor-made programs that contribute to the growth of Blue Economy particularly for developing countries through contributions to capacity building and bridging knowledge gaps which help their economic growth objectives. This can be achieved through partnerships among education and scientific institutions of other countries and regions.

Seventh, innovation and entrepreneurship are important facets for the development of Blue Economy and the SMEs, entrepreneurs and startups act as catalyst for the sustainable use of oceans which would potentially turn into job creation. These often find it difficult to organize requisite finances to turn their ideas into operations. The governments are cautious of sharing finances with private agencies / individuals and prefer government bodies and institutions to provide financial support for research and development. Besides, such financial support is often prone to bureaucratic hurdles.

There are a number of ways available to raise funds such as long and short term capital through venture capitalists who prefer technology-driven businesses and companies with high-growth potential in areas such as information technology, communications, and biotechnology; Angels are those people who are generally wealthy or retired company executives who want to invest directly in small firms; and business incubators provide financial support for new businesses in various stages of development.

Eighth, Foreign Direct Investment which is focused on the oceans can help in technology transfer, promote research, and industrial development, skill enhancement resulting in innovative technological solutions and pioneering products, services and jobs.

Ninth, companies, investors, and end users need to network, which can potentially encourage entrepreneurship and start-ups to adopt an integrated approach to the development of Blue Economy

Tenth, the role of women in the development of Blue Economy through SMEs, innovation and empowerment merits consideration. Their engagement results in growth in domestic income and social and economic prosperity.

Finally, as the global community works towards harnessing the Blue Economy, which demands newer ways to manage the oceans and its resources, it is important to obtain a better understanding of not only the seas and the oceans, but also develop systems, processes and methodologies through technology, skills and entrepreneurship.

Appendix

Sustainable Development Goal 14 (SDG14)-Goals, targets and specific indicators

Goal 14. Conserve and sustainably use the oceans, seas and marine resources for sustainable development

Target 14.1 By 2025, prevent and significantly reduce marine pollution of all kinds, in particular from land-based activities, including marine debris and nutrient pollution.

Indicator 14.1.1: Index of coastal eutrophication and floating plastic debris density

Target 14.2 By 2020, sustainably manage and protect marine and coastal ecosystems to avoid significant adverse impacts, including by strengthening their resilience, and take action for their restoration in order to achieve healthy and productive oceans.

Indicator 14.2.1: Proportion of national exclusive economic zones managed using ecosystem-based approaches

Target 14.3 Minimize and address the impacts of ocean acidification, including through enhanced scientific cooperation at all levels

Indicator 14.3.1 Average marine acidity (pH) measured at agreed suite of representative sampling stations

Target 14.4 By 2020, effectively regulate harvesting and end overfishing, illegal, unreported and unregulated fishing and destructive fishing practices and implement science-based management plans, in order to restore fish stocks in the shortest time feasible, at least to levels that can produce maximum sustainable yield as determined by their biological characteristics

Indicator 14.4.1 Proportion of fish stocks within biologically sustainable levels

Target 14.5 By 2020, conserve at least 10 per cent of coastal and marine areas, consistent with national and international law and based on the best available scientific information

Indicator 14.5.1 Coverage of protected areas in relation to marine areas

Target 14.6 By 2020, prohibit certain forms of fisheries subsidies which contribute to overcapacity and overfishing, eliminate subsidies that contribute to illegal, unreported and unregulated fishing and refrain from introducing new such subsidies, recognizing that appropriate and effective special and differential treatment for developing and least developed countries should be an integral part of the World Trade Organization fisheries subsidies negotiation[1]

Indicator 14.6.1 Progress by countries in the degree of implementation of international instruments aiming to combat illegal, unreported and unregulated fishing

Target 14.7 By 2030, increase the economic benefits to small island developing States and least developed countries from the sustainable use of marine resources, including through sustainable management of fisheries, aquaculture and tourism

Indicator 14.7.1 Sustainable fisheries as a percentage of GDP in small island developing States, least developed countries and all countries

Target 14.a Increase scientific knowledge, develop research capacity and transfer marine technology, taking into account the Intergovernmental Oceanographic Commission Criteria and Guidelines on the Transfer of Marine Technology, in order to improve ocean health and to enhance the contribution of marine biodiversity to the development of developing countries, in particular small island developing States and least developed countries

Indicator 14.a.1 Proportion of total research budget allocated to research in the field of marine technology

Target 14.b Provide access for small-scale artisanal fishers to marine resources and markets

Indicator 14.b.1 Progress by countries in the degree of application of a legal/regulatory/policy/institutional framework which recognizes and protects access rights for small-scale fisheries

Target 14.c Enhance the conservation and sustainable use of oceans and their

---

1   Taking into account ongoing World Trade Organization negotiations, the Doha Development Agenda and the Hong Kong ministerial mandate.

resources by implementing international law as reflected in the United Nations Convention on the Law of the Sea, which provides the legal framework for the conservation and sustainable use of oceans and their resources, as recalled in paragraph 158 of "The future we want"

Indicator 14.c.1 Number of countries making progress in ratifying, accepting and implementing through legal, policy and institutional frameworks, ocean-related instruments that implement international law, as reflected in the United Nation Convention on the Law of the Sea, for the conservation and sustainable use of the oceans and their resources.

Perth Principles

Declaration of the Indian Ocean Rim Association on the principles for peaceful, productive and sustainable use of the Indian Ocean and its resources

WE, the Foreign Ministers of the Member States of the Indian Ocean Rim Association (IORA), Australia, Bangladesh, Comoros, India, Indonesia, Iran, Kenya, Madagascar, Malaysia, Mauritius, Mozambique, Oman, Seychelles, Singapore, South Africa, Sri Lanka, Tanzania, Thailand, United Arab Emirates and Yemen, on the occasion of the thirteenth Council of Ministers' Meeting (COMM)

1. **REITERATING** that IORA is the apex pan-regional organisation for the Indian Ocean.

2. **RECALLING** the six priority areas of cooperation agreed at the eleventh COMM in Bengaluru, namely: Maritime Safety and Security; Trade and Investment Facilitation; Fisheries Management; Disaster Risk Management; Academic and Science and Technology Cooperation; and Tourism and Cultural Exchanges.

3. **RECALLING ALSO** our desire to promote the sustainable growth and balanced development of the Indian Ocean region and IORA Member States, and to create common ground for regional economic cooperation.

4. **COMMITTED** to promoting cooperation and collaboration between IORA and other Indian Ocean regional stakeholders including Dialogue Partner States and other regional and international forums.

5. **REAFFIRMING** our commitment to the Charter of the United Nations, to the Charter of IORA, and to the applicable principles of international law.

6. **REAFFIRMING** ALSO our commitment to 'The Future We Want',

as adopted at the 2012 United Nation as Conference on Sustainable Development, and to the protection, restoration, health, productivity and resilience of the Indian Ocean and its resources.

7. **RECOGNISING** that the United Nations Convention on the Law of the Sea provides the legal framework for the conservation and sustainable use of the oceans and their resources and plays a vital role in maintaining peaceful cooperation and stability across the Indian Ocean.

HEREBY DECLARE AS FOLLOWS:

That the Member States of IORA are guided by the following principles for productive and sustainable use of the Indian Ocean and its resources:

1. Recognition of the importance of the Indian Ocean's biodiversity, including its marine life and ecosystems.

2. Commitment to the conservation and sustainable use of the Indian Ocean and its resources in accordance with international law, including fisheries stocks, water and seabed resources and other marine life; and commitment to deliver on the economic, social and environmental dimensions of sustainable development.

3. Recognition of the important contribution of the conservation and sustainable use of the Indian Ocean and its resources to poverty eradication, sustained economic growth, food security and creation of sustainable livelihoods and decent work.

4. Recognition of the importance of building the capacity of countries to conserve, sustainably manage and realise the benefits of sustainable fisheries.

5. Commitment to intensify efforts, individually and collectively, to take the measures necessary to maintain or restore all fish stocks to levels that can produce the maximum sustainable yield.

6. Commitment to understand and address the main threats to the Indian Ocean and its resources, including illegal, unreported and unregulated

fishing, unsustainable fishing practices, loss of critical coastal ecosystems and the adverse impacts of pollution, ocean acidification, marine debris, and invasive species on the marine environment.

7. Recognition of the importance of building the capacity of countries to understand, forecast and address marine, ocean and climate science issues in the Indian Ocean.

ADOPTED by the Foreign Ministers of the Member States of the Indian Ocean Rim Association on 1 November 2013 in Perth, Australia.

Perth

November 1st, 2013

Blue Economy, Abu Dhabi Declaration, 2014

We, the participating Heads of State and Government and high-level representatives, having met in Abu Dhabi, United Arab Emirates, from 19 to 20 January 2014, held as part of the Abu Dhabi Sustainability Week and in preparation for the Third International Conference on Small Island Developing States in Apia, Samoa in September 2014, with the participation of civil society, discussed how to utilise and implement the Blue Economy as a tool to enable the transition of development models for island and coastal States towards sustainable development.

Noting that the Blue Economy, founded in line with the concept and principles of, and mutually supportive with the Green Economy, is a tool that offers specific mechanisms for Small Island Developing States (SIDS) and coastal countries to address their sustainable development challenges.

Recognising the significant contribution that the Blue Economy can make towards the alleviation of hunger, poverty eradication, creation of sustainable livelihoods and mitigation of climate change.

Cognisant of the fundamental importance of the marine environment and its resources to future, inclusive sustainable development – *inter alia*:

> ➤ Fisheries and their vital role in providing food security and sustainable livelihoods,

> ➤ Tourism as a source of decent employment and a contributor to poverty alleviation,

> ➤ As a source of renewable energy from wind, wave, tidal, thermal and biomass sources.

> ➤ As a source of hydrocarbon and mineral resources.

> ➤ As the primary medium of global trade through shipping and port facilities.

Aware and greatly concerned that the oceans of the world are threatened and being seriously degraded by unsustainable exploitation, pollution, habitat destruction and acidification and being determined to address these threats.

Welcoming the report of the Regional Preparatory Meeting of Small Island Developing States of the Atlantic Indian Ocean, Mediterranean and South China Seas held in Seychelles from 17-19 July 2013.

Welcoming the report of the Nairobi Convention Regional Workshop on: Contributions of Natural Blue Capital to a Green Economy, held in Seychelles 11-13 December 2013.

Recognising that States should take efforts to enhance management mechanisms that minimise and mitigate unsustainable exploitation of marine resources.

Recognising that for many States transition to a Blue Economy will entail a fundamental, systemic change in policy, legal and governance frameworks.

Noting that enabling mechanisms for the Blue Economy include technology transfer, capacity building, targeted streamlined financing mechanisms, including debt for nature and/or adaptation swaps, and modes of science-based implementation.

Recalling that the United Nations Conference on Sustainable Development in Rio de Janeiro, June 2012, recognised the need for significant mobilisation of resources from a variety of sources and the effective use of financing, in order to give strong support to developing countries in their efforts to promote sustainable development.

Notes that the Blue Economy offers significant applications and benefits by offering a framework to protect and enhance the value of marine and coastal systems through an integrated approach.

Stresses the importance of enhanced mechanisms for governance of the high seas.

Reaffirms the integral importance of cooperation, both national and international, including civil society organisations and their further empowerment in the sustainable development of our seas and oceans.

Underscores that the Blue Economy is founded upon research, assessment and data sharing, and that the assessment and valuation of the blue capital will require diverse and strong scientific and technical capacities.

Urges the further development of an integrated ecosystem approach to the maintenance of balanced, healthy and productive marine ecosystems, including the valuation of blue capital and potential applications of "blue carbon" trading.

Urges States, international agencies and donors to develop means to support and facilitate the implementation of the Blue Economy in developing countries.

Calls for prompt action in the further development of the Blue Economy concept that, drawing from and building upon existing initiatives, mainstreams and enables the Blue Economy concept as a distinct tool on the international sustainable development agenda.

Express our appreciation to the government of the United Arab Emirates for its hosting of this Summit.

First Blue Economy Dialogue

GOA DECLARATION

The First IORA Blue Economy Dialogue was held in Goa, India on 17-18, August 2015. The dialogue deliberated key aspects of Blue Economy that included an accounting framework; fisheries & aquaculture; renewable ocean energy; ports, shipping and manufacturing services; and sea-bed explorations and minerals. Major highlights of the Dialogue included:

Accounting Framework

*   Blue Economy paradigm envisages a development strategy aimed at economic growth, environmental sustainability, that focuses on poverty alleviation, job-creation and social equity.

*   That a global consensus on a precise definition of Blue Economy is still emerging. This pertains to a framework that accounts for Blue Economy covering ocean economy, coastal economy, and marine economy besides the governmental sectors.

*   An appropriate sectoral classification for accounting framework is critical in estimating the size of the Blue Economy. Besides inclusion of sectors, their geographical locations are significant in identifying Blue Economy activities. A suitable sectoral classification should therefore be identified to account for the Blue Economies of the IORA Member states and the region as a whole.

*   That some IORA countries have legislated upon National Ocean Acts. It facilitates federal budgeting for the development of Blue Economy activities. It may be recognised that there is diversity of budgetary practices in different Member countries which should be considered suitably in the accounting framework. These initiatives could encourage Member countries to adopt a focussed approach towards promoting Blue Economy.

*   Given the asymmetry that exists among the Member countries with regard to Blue Economy accounting norms, a commonly agreed

regional approach, including constituting a regional agency, would help in this regard.

- Setting up of a task-force to work out the definitional issues and measures to estimate Blue Economies of the Member states and the region as whole.

Fisheries and Aquaculture

- It is recognised that fisheries and aquaculture are the drivers of Blue Economy in the region. It provides food, nutrition and employment opportunities to the people in the region.

- Overfishing, illegal, unreported and unregulated (IUU) fishing, bycatches and fishing in the high seas remain key challenges to the fisheries and aquaculture in the region.

- Region's fishery sector is also subjected to market-access constraints on account of Non-Tariff Barriers (NTBs), Sanitary and Phyto-sanitary (SPS), and Technical Barriers to Trade (TBT) in the developed and emerging countries markets.

- That fisheries exports have remained at sub-optimum levels on account of recessionary pressures of the world economy causing the terms of the trade to deteriorate further, especially, for the low-income countries.

- Sustainable exploitation of fishery resources can be enhanced with enforcement of precautionary instruments such as catch quota, marine protected areas, constant monitoring, etc among others. Implementation of such policies can ensure sustainability of fish production and consumption in the region. The region is also facing pressing issues like subsidies, license fees, generation of revenues for RFMOs, breach on international and regional conventions, etc. where regional regulatory mechanism may be warranted.

- Fish processing industry in the Member countries may be promoted for higher value creation, better remuneration to fish farmers and enriching nutrition content.

- For effective governance of fisheries, a regional institutional mechanism may be evolved to enforce commonly agreed principles on individual Member countries.

Renewable Ocean Energy

- Renewable ocean energy generated from wind, solar, tidal and other sources could play an important role in supplementing growing energy demand in the region.

- Harnessing renewable energy resources requires substantial investment and capacity building. Some Member countries are better off than others in attracting resources to the renewable energy sectors.

- Member countries may set up industrial clusters specific to ocean energy to promote inter-industry learning so as to co-evolve the production chain and technology for cost minimization and promoting indigenization.

- Joint collaboration between domestic and foreign firms may enhance efforts for technology development, resource assessment and choice of appropriate technologies.

- There is a need to develop off-shore environmental governance system to minimise conflicts and competition between different sectors.

Ports, Shipping and Other Manufacturing Services

- Ports, shipping, marine biotechnology, multi-specie aquaculture etc. are some of the emerging Blue Economy sectors in the region.

- The Member countries can develop their shipping services by acquiring new ships to replace ageing ships; building port infrastructure including setting up of large floating structures which can be used for transhipment or entertainment activities, developing mega hub ports, etc. There is potential to promote ship repairing services in different Member countries to serve the need of such services in the Indian Ocean.

- Coastal tourism can be promoted by acquisition of cruise liners having an intra-country cruise liner sea circuit, sharing management best practices; setting up of an Indian Ocean Sea tourism Board, etc.

- Indian Ocean region is rich in biodiversity with a number of biological hotspots including coral reefs. The chance of finding novel molecules with high therapeutic potential is very high.

- Marine organisms in the Indian Ocean could be used for development of pharmaceuticals. Several drugs have already been tested and marketed using ocean resources. This sector may be promoted for commercialization of drugs with private sector participation.

Sea-bed Exploration and Minerals

- Sea-bed minerals such as hydrocarbon, polymetallic nodules, ferromanganese crusts, hydrothermal sulphides, rare earth metals etc are important to the region.

- A comprehensive Ocean policy for exploration of minerals as well as energy sources may facilitate regional cooperation in the region.

- Sharing of technology may be initiated to fill technology gaps and exchange of expertise for exploration in the deep sea.

- Regional Economic Communities (RECs) which involve IORA Member states also need to be sensitized through institutional dialogue.

- Spatial clarity is necessary in order for countries around the Indian Ocean to understand and enforce their rights and obligations.

- Development of sea-bed resources should be taken up in tandem with environmental guidelines issued by international agencies such as IMO, ISA, etc.

- There should be a dialogue within IORA to develop consensus on the above mentioned issues.

21 Aug 2015

IORA

Mauritius Declaration on Blue Economy

Declaration of the Indian Ocean Rim Association on Enhancing Blue Economy Cooperation for Sustainable Development in the Indian Ocean Region.

WE, the Ministers and representatives of the Member States of the Indian Ocean Rim Association (hereinafter referred to as "IORA"), Australia, Bangladesh, Comoros, India, Indonesia, Kenya, Madagascar, Mauritius, Mozambique, Sultanate of Oman, Seychelles, Singapore, South Africa, Sri Lanka, Tanzania, Thailand and United Arab Emirates attended the First IORA Ministerial Blue Economy Conference in Mauritius on 2 – 3 September 2015;

- RECOGNISING the importance of the Blue Economy vis-a-vis :

  - ➤ **Fisheries and Aquaculture** to ensure food security and contribute to poverty alleviation and sustainable livelihoods;

  - ➤ **Renewable Ocean Energy** to reduce the cost of energy and to mitigate and adapt to the impact of climate change;

  - ➤ **Seaport and Shipping** to promote trade, investment and maritime connectivity in the Indian Ocean Rim region; and,

  - ➤ **Offshore Hydrocarbons and Seabed Minerals** to foster new business opportunities and attract investment in the Indian Ocean;

- RECOGNISING the need of Member States and Dialogue Partners to promote proper management of marine resources and enhance capacity building in developing countries, Small Island Developing States (SIDS) and Least Developed Countries (LDCs);

- REAFFIRMING IORA's role to promote collaboration and cooperation in the Blue Economy for balanced economic development among IORA Member States and Dialogue Partners;

- **ENCOURAGING** IORA Member States and Dialogue Partners to enhance capacity for the protection of coastal areas, marine environment and resources to ensure sustainable development in the Indian Ocean Rim region;

- **RECALLING** the Rio +20 United Nations Conference on Sustainable Development held in Rio de Janeiro, Brazil on 20 - 22 June 2012, that integrates social, economic and environmental goals and objectives for decision-making;

- **RECALLING** the IORA Perth Principles for peaceful, productive and sustainable use of the Indian Ocean and its resources agreed by IORA Ministers in Perth, Australia on 1 November 2013; and the IORA Economic Declaration adopted by IORA Ministers in Perth on 9 October 2014 which recognized the blue economy is emerging as a common source of growth, innovation and job creation for the Indian Ocean Region;

- **RECALLING** the establishment of the Blue Economy Core Group and the conduct of the preparatory workshops for the First IORA Ministerial Blue Economy Conference (BEC) including: (i) The IORA Blue Economy Core Group Workshop on "Promoting Fisheries & Aquaculture and Maritime Safety & Security Cooperation in Indian Ocean Region" that was held in Durban, South Africa, on 4 - 5 May 2015; (ii) The Indian Ocean Region Workshop on "Exploration and Development of Seabed Minerals and Hydrocarbons: Current Capability and Emerging Science Needs" that took place in Bali, Indonesia from 26 - 27 July 2015 and (iii) the IORA Dialogue on the Blue Economy in Goa, India on 17-18 August, 2015;

- **RECALLING** the Third International Conference on Financing for Development that was held in Addis Ababa, Ethiopia, from 13-16 July 2015 that holistically looked at financing for development across three dimensions and addressed the way in which inclusive growth and sustainable development can be achieved to address issues including sustainable energy; climate change; disaster risk reduction; oceans and seas; food security and nutrition; sustainable transportation; gender equality and women's empowerment; and, biodiversity;

- **RECOGNISING** the importance of the proposed Sustainable Development Goals (SDGs) for the Blue Economy, especially for the conservation and sustainable use of the oceans, seas and marine resources for development;

- **RECALLING** IORA's commitment to develop a common vision in making the Blue Economy an engine for sustainable development and sound environmental management in the Indian Ocean Region;

- **RECONFIRMING** IORA's belief in promoting an innovative and sustainable Blue Economy in the Indian Ocean Region;

- **COMMITTING** to an optimization of the populations' benefit from the economic activity of the ocean;

- **REITTERATING** the importance of IORA's cooperation and engagement with Dialogue Partners, relevant international and regional organizations, the private sector, and civil society in delivering Blue Economy objectives;

HEREBY DECLARE AS FOLLOWS:

That the Member States of IORA will be guided by the following principles in our shared goal to foster the sustainable development of the Blue Economy in the Indian Ocean Region:

- The Blue Economy paradigm is founded on the ecosystem approach, including science-based conservation of marine resources and ecosystems, as a means to realise sustainable development;

- IORA's priority sectors of the Blue Economy, including: Fisheries and Aquaculture; Renewable Ocean Energy; Seaports and Shipping; and Offshore Hydrocarbons and Seabed Minerals that should be developed in an environmentally sound manner for the socio-economic benefit of the population;

- Sustainable use of marine resources of the Indian Ocean should be carried out according to international law including UNCLOS and the Convention on Biological Diversity;

- Member States are also encouraged to consider formulating measures for the development of the Blue Economy in a sustainable manner;

- Cooperation by IORA Member States on data collection and development of environmental baselines could ensure a strong foundation for informed decision making and policy development;

- IORA Member States shall promote sustainable fisheries including combating Illegal Unreported and Unregulated (IUU) fishing;

- The role of the IORA Blue Economy Core Group that will focus on: Fisheries and Aquaculture; Renewable Ocean Energy; Seaports and Shipping; and Offshore Hydrocarbons and Seabed Minerals; to promote the Blue Economy as a driver for sustainable development; research and development; investment, technology transfer and capacity building should be encouraged so as to explore the full potential of the oceans and to ensure sustainable development in the Indian Ocean Rim region;

- IORA Member States should attach higher importance on the sustainable development of the Blue Economy and be encouraged to strengthen networking, the exchange of experiences and best practices in relation to the development of the Blue Economy in the Indian Ocean Rim region;

- Member States and Dialogue Partners should be encouraged to facilitate and allocate the availability of sufficient funding from all sources to promote mutual cooperation and technology transfer with regards to the sustainable development of the Blue Economy in the Indian Ocean Rim Region;

- The sustainable development of the IORA priority sectors of the Blue Economy in the Indian Ocean Region would contribute to: food security; poverty alleviation; the mitigation of and resilience to the impacts of climate change; enhanced trade and investment; enhanced maritime connectivity; economic diversification; job creation and socio- economic growth;

- The empowerment of women and facilitation of micro, small and medium enterprises to participate in the development of the Blue Economy is essential to equitable and sustainable economic growth;

- Improving research, networking, and promoting researchers' exchange programmes among the Member States and Dialogue Partners is vital to ensure sustained development in the region: taking advantage of the upcoming UNESCO Indian Ocean Expedition II (IOEII) as endorsed by the 2014 Perth Communique;

- The need to involve Public-Private Partnership to enhance productivity and marketing efforts in different sectors of the Blue Economy;

- The need to set-up or revise existing regional regulatory frameworks and governance with regard to development of the Blue Economy in the region, drawing upon existing case studies and experience where it exists;

- The participation of Multilateral Organisations can make a valuable contribution to the sustainable development of the Blue Economy;

- Blue Economy development in Member States would create a conducive business environment and attract foreign investment to boost growth;

- Member States and Dialogue Partners should promote capacity building for the development of professional skills for the sustainable development and sound environmental management of different sectors in the Blue Economy.

ADOPTED by the Blue Economy Ministers and Senior Officials of the Member States of the Indian Ocean Rim Association on 03 September 2015 in Mauritius.

Abu Dhabi 2016

Blue Economy Declaration

We, the participating Heads of State and Government and high-level representatives, having met in Abu Dhabi, United Arab Emirates, on the 19 January 2016, held as part of the Abu Dhabi Sustainability Week with the participation of representatives from international organizations, business and civil society, including representatives of our youth, discussed how to develop and apply the Blue Economy approach to support the implementation of the Paris Agreement on Climate Change and the realisation of all relevant Sustainable Development Goals and particularly Goal 14 and its related targets.

Recalling the 2014 Abu Dhabi Declaration on the Blue Economy.

Reaffirming that the Blue Economy, founded in line with and mutually supportive of the concept of the Green Economy, is a productive approach to the sustainable management of our seas and the ocean and thereby a significant contribution to the alleviation of global poverty, creation of sustainable livelihoods, increased food and nutrition security, improved human well-being and social equity, accompanied by reduced environmental risks and ecological scarcities.

Noting that elements of the Blue Economy include *inter alia* several key elements for the mitigation of climate change, such as the protection and restoration of carbon sinks in coastal and marine ecosystems, the development of low-carbon clean technologies applied to the marine environment, greater use of marine renewable energy, and also include significant reduction of major ocean pollutants, and changes towards more sustainable fisheries and aquaculture management regimes.

Welcoming the adoption of United Nations General Assembly Resolution 70/1: "Transforming our world: the 2030 Agenda for Sustainable Development", in particular its Goal 14, and

Noting that the Blue Economy is supportive of several of the Sustainable Development Goals but relates particularly to Goal 14: "Conserve and sustainably use the oceans, seas and marine resources for sustainable development" which in effect provides a mandate for the Blue Economy paradigm.

Reiterating Resolution 70/1's call for, and commitment to a revitalized Global Partnership as a means to ensure the implementation of the 2030 Agenda and its SDGs, including Goal 14.

Further recalling and welcoming Resolution (70/226) of the UNGA to organise a United Nations Conference to Support the Implementation of Sustainable Development Goal 14, to be co-hosted by the Governments of Fiji and Sweden in June 2017.

Welcoming the historic Paris Agreement under the United Nations Framework Convention on Climate Change recognising the ocean as an essential part of the climate system and therefore a part of the solution for building climate change resilience.

Noting that the Paris Agreement calls for the mobilisation of climate finance for both mitigation and adaptation to be scaled up and represent a progression beyond previous efforts.

Recalling the UN general Assembly endorsement of the Addis Ababa Action Agenda of the third International Conference on Financing for Development which provides a new global framework for financing sustainable development.

Recognising the vital role the oceans play in supporting life on earth and the mitigation of climate change and being aware of the scale of the on-going degradation of marine ecosystems and their biodiversity that is threatening the ocean's capacity to fulfil these roles. Also recognising the vital role oceans play in global trade.

Further recognising the urgent need for coastal nations to move toward an integrated, ecosystem-based approach in their management of marine resources that links key issues and challenges across jurisdictional and political boundaries, supported by management tools such as marine spatial planning, and acts as as a fundamental precursor for inclusive sustainable development and the mitigation of climate change.

Underlining that sustainable local fisheries, including small scale fisheries and those of special cultural and socioeconomic significance, represent the first step towards developing the Blue Economy within developing nations, we resolve to further foster support and financing opportunities for local fishery entrepreneurs and especially communities dependant on the sea, within the context of inclusive sustainable management plans and marine spatial plans to combat and reduce illegal, unreported and unregulated fishing.

Recalling that science and sustained ocean observations are essential for understanding and assessing the role and potential value of healthy marine and coastal ecosystems and that they should underpin Blue Economy development so as to enhance the benefits of marine and coastal ecosystems through an integrated and inclusive approach.

Also emphasising the need for broad international and regional cooperation in the maintenance of and recovery to healthy and productive marine ecosystems and the sustainable development of our seas.

Highlighting the need for the mobilisation and effective use of new, additional and diverse resources through streamlined mechanisms to support human and institutional capacity building, including transfer of marine technology, on mutually agreed terms, and innovative approaches to all of these.

Urge States, international agencies and donors to take concerted action and facilitate the application of the Blue Economy in the realisation of the Sustainable Development Goals and implementation of the Paris Agreement on Climate Change, including through public-private partnerships.

Express our appreciation to the Governments of the United Arab Emirates and Seychelles, and the Intergovernmental Oceanographic Commission of UNESCO for their co-hosting of this Summit.

Index

www.ingramcontent.com/pod-product-compliance
Lightning Source LLC
Chambersburg PA
CBHW031550260326
41914CB00002B/350